SECRET PHOENIX

A GUIDE TO THE WEIRD, WONDERFUL, AND OBSCURE

Christine K. Bailey

Library of Congress Control Number: 2017934672

ISBN: 9781681060729

Design by Jill Halpin

Printed in the United States of America

17 18 19 20 21 5 4 3 2 1

CONTENTS

INTRODUCTION

Welcome to *Secret Phoenix*, where you'll discover the forgotten and even missing pieces of a desert metropolis. In a transient city like Phoenix, the oral tradition has been left lacking, but people scattered across the Salt River Valley (also known as Valley of the Sun, or "the Valley," for short) have made it their life's work to capture these golden nuggets of our past before they disappear forever. Within these pages, you'll read the stories of some of our oddest and most iconic buildings, the legends of our more notorious criminals, and the explanations for the various odds and ends that seem as out of place, as say . . . an anchor in the middle of the desert. Whether you're a newcomer who plans to stay, a seasonal tourist, or even a native Phoenician who wants to learn a little more about a city you've grown to love, you will walk away full of fun, quirky, interesting, and seemingly irrelevant facts that will begin to form for you a reason for our being—the story of our journey as a city from a little cow town to the sixth-largest city in the United States. Just as Arizona was once called the "Baby State" (in 2012, we celebrated 100 years of statehood), Phoenix is still a young'un, and as it evolves beyond its adolescence, it will continue to leave in its wake a rich and storied past and an ever more complicated present. In the months it took to research, write, and photograph these various obscure, hidden, and sometimes misremembered stories, I discovered that many more secrets and many more unexplained pieces are waiting to be unearthed. I hope you enjoy the ones I have recorded within these pages and that this book inspires you to keep your eye out for more.

ACKNOWLEDGMENTS

This book was a labor of love, but not just mine. It was made possible because of the local historians, experts, journalists, and writers who found it important to rescue from the wheels of time's forward movement the pieces and parts of our fluid past. They have captured our history and nailed it down in books, photographs, and articles (both print and online) so that when we finally slow down and look back we'll have something to see, something that tells us where we came from and how we got to where we are today.

Thank you especially to the following individuals listed alphabetically: Bluebird, Vic Linoff, Frank McGuire, Marshall Shore, Jon Talton, and Marshall Trimble, who have graciously shared with an excited, but somewhat naïve writer what they had already discovered: too much of our Phoenix history is lost; any piece that's left is worth fighting to save; and the power of preservation comes from pausing to share what we know with one another—whether by pen, email, or in person. Thank you for helping me capture a little piece of the puzzle. Your time, wisdom, and insight were invaluable in helping me navigate the past. The errors here are mine. I hope I have preserved a small part of what makes Phoenix and its surrounding cities special.

And to my husband, Matt, whose labor of love meant driving me all over the Valley so that I could record each of these stories with a camera. I love you.

A MYSTERIOUS TREAT

Where can I get a date shake?

Like the Sonoran dog, the date shake is one of Arizona's interesting interpretations of Americana—a frothy milk shake mixed with a unique, desert ingredient: the date, but the dates and the trees from which they originated were not indigenous to Arizona. While towering palms have become synonymous with the Valley resorts and skyline, they did not arrive here on their own. They were brought from other similar regions in the world, including the Middle East. The date palm arrived sometime in the 1920s, but then something quite strange happened: a seedling appeared. A man by the name of Roy Franklin recognized it as a new variety and began harvesting the dates in the Arcadia neighborhood of Phoenix. While not one of the state's Five Cs (Arizona's Five Cs are the five foundational components of the state's economy: citrus, cattle, copper, climate, and cotton), date farming became part of the area's agricultural makeup. The new dates were named "Sphinx" to account for their mysterious appearance, and the industry took off.

Today, the Black Sphinx date is only found in Phoenix and continues to be harvested from the remaining trees in Arcadia. If you drive down 44th Street and look west, you'll see a group of towering palms. These are the remaining black date palm trees and the site of the original 47-acre Sphinx Date Ranch. The Sphinx Date in Scottsdale still harvests its black dates from these trees.

The Black Sphinx date is also known as the Black Phoenix.

The Sphinx Date Co. Palm Pantry on Scottsdale Road.

The Sphinx Date Co. sells other local treats, such as saguaro syrup. You can purchase these items online or in-store at the Sphinx Date Co. Palm & Pantry in Scottsdale.

DATE SHAKE

WHAT A tasty treat

WHERE 3039 N. Scottsdale Road, Scottsdale, Arizona

COST A few dollars

PRO TIP The date shake is made with Medjool dates rather than the rarer Black Phoenix.

2 A FREEMASON'S HEADSTONE

Who is buried under the white pyramid at Papago Park?

If you see a flash of something reflective and white among the red rocks of Papago Park, it is most likely Hunt's Tomb. The tiled white pyramid perched above the Phoenix Zoo at Papago Park is the final resting place of Arizona's first governor, George W. P. Hunt, known at one time as Arizona's "Grand Old Man." He served seven terms as governor before he was laid to rest with one of the best views in the Valley. Why a pyramid? Some say Hunt was a Freemason, and the pyramid held special meaning. Others say he became fascinated by the pyramids after a trip to Egypt. Either way, in 1931, when his wife, Helen, died, Hunt had her memorial built as a pyramid. He later joined Helen after his own death a few years later in 1934. According to the *Arizona Republic*, Hunt was a man dedicated to "growing up with the West." He built a connection with the people of Arizona first in the mines and later as a waiter in restaurants in the mining town of Globe. When it came time to campaign for Arizona's first gubernatorial seat, Hunt reached out

---

Also entombed at Papago Park are Hunt's daughter, Virginia, and Helen's mother, father, and sister.

Top: Tourists take in the view near Hunt's Tomb.
Left: Hunt's Tomb gleams in the sun at Papago Park.

to the men and women he knew "growing up" in the territory. On his inauguration day, it is said that he walked the several blocks to the capitol building rather than ride in his buggy. In his seven terms as governor, he worked to get children ages eight to fourteen in school, eliminate child labor, and create old age pensions. Today, the pyramid stands as a monument to his life and role in building Arizona.

HUNT'S TOMB

WHAT A tomb

WHERE Papago Park, 625 N. Galvin Pkwy., Phoenix, Arizona

COST Free

PRO TIP Hunt chose his location well; the site offers a spectacular view of the surrounding cities—Tempe and Phoenix.

BIRTHPLACE OF A RELIGION

Is Phoenix the birthplace of Scientology?

Author and philosopher L. Ron Hubbard lived in Phoenix when he began writing the lectures and books that would become the foundation for the Church of Scientology. Hubbard moved to Phoenix in 1952 and soon after began giving lectures at what was then called the Phoenix Little Theatre off Central Avenue and McDowell Road adjacent to the Phoenix Art Museum. He lived in a house that you can still see near 44th Street and Camelback Road. The desert-landscaped home served as his retreat, and today it is considered a museum to the man and his teachings. Only members can visit the house, but the public can visit the Church of Scientology's Public Information Center. Located about a mile from Hubbard's home at 44th Street and Indianola, it features a history of Scientology, Dianetics, and the man behind them.

The Church of Scientology in Phoenix opened in 2012.

The Church of Scientology at 44th Street and Indianola in Phoenix.

CHURCH OF SCIENTOLOGY

WHAT A church

WHERE 3875 N. 44th St., Phoenix, Arizona

COST Free

PRO TIP The visitor center demonstrates how the religion has evolved.

4 CHANDLER'S BASEMENT-COME-SPEAKEASY

Was Chandler's new speakeasy just a giant storage closet?

The unassuming set of stairs across the street from the San Tan Brewery doesn't seem like much, but after 6:00 p.m. most nights it provides access to one of the Valley's handful of secret speakeasies. The owners of Crust, the restaurant above, discovered the space when they began renovating the southeast corner of the San Marcos Resort. One of the Valley's latest craft-cocktail restaurants, The Ostrich was once the basement of the San Marcos, complete with tunnels that flooded, tales of Prohibition-era speakeasies, and even a ghost story or two. History points to a less-exciting past—the basement served as a storage room for A. J. Chandler's vast collection of ostrich feathers. Dr. Chandler was the founder of the city and the resort, which opened in 1914. He was convinced that ostriches and their flapper-era feathers were an ideal investment and stored them for the next couple of decades. Today, the old basement, with its exposed brick walls and ceiling,

The Ostrich is open 6:00 p.m.–2:00 a.m. Tuesday–Saturday.

The basement-level entrance to the Ostrich.

wrought iron-gated liquor closet, antique-style furniture, and old photos evokes the spirit of the 1920s and '30s, and whispers of secret speakeasies are enough to inspire folks to embrace the bar's tawdrier tales. To cap it off, it serves some of the best craft cocktails in the East Valley. The drink menu runs the gamut from old favorites, such as manhattans, sazeracs, and Singapore Slings, to newly minted concoctions from the bar's team of expert mixologists.

THE OSTRICH

WHAT An underground speakeasy

WHERE 10 North San Marcos Place, Chandler, Arizona

COST The price of a drink

PRO TIP The food menu matches the drink menu— old favorites and the newly imagined.

11

HORSEWORLD

Where can I see an Arabian horse, a quarter horse, a thoroughbred, and a mustang all in the same place?

Ranching, cowboys, and wild mustangs have always been a part of Arizona's heritage, but Arabian stallions are another thing entirely. They are the oldest and finest of the purebreds, and a win in Scottsdale has come to mean big money for breeders around the world. Since 1955 the annual Scottsdale Arabian Horse Show has grown from a mere 50 horses hosted at the Arizona Biltmore to almost 2,400 horses at the 400-acre WestWorld of Scottsdale. Owned and operated by the City of Scottsdale, WestWorld hosts more than a hundred shows a year. It's also one of the only places in town where you can see just about every type of horse. Besides the Arabian Horse Show, it is also home to the annual Bentley Polo Match, the Arizona Quarter Horse Championship, and the well-known Barrett-Jackson Auto Show, where you can probably find at least one Mustang.

At the entrance to WestWorld off Pima Road, *Horseworld*, a life-size bronze sculpture, welcomes hundreds of thousands of visitors a year. The bronze piece is the work of sculptor Snell Johnson; and it displays each of the three horses most often found at WestWorld—an Arabian, a quarter horse, and a thoroughbred. Each is doing what he does best. The thoroughbred is racing, the Arabian is

---

WestWorld installed local artist Jeff Zischke's larger-than-life sculpture *Impulsion* in 2014.

Horseworld *at the entrance to WestWorld of Scottsdale.*

showing, and the American quarter horse is cutting (or separating a single cow from the herd).

6 THOUSANDS OF ACRES OF CITY PARK

Where can I visit one of the largest city parks in the country?

One of the largest city parks in the country is hidden in a lengthy stretch of Sonoran Desert along the southern edge of Phoenix. The massive 16,000-acre park is not a state or federal park but a city park and preserve encompassing three separate mountain ranges. It accounts for almost half of the 40,000 acres of city park in Phoenix proper. The park is longer than it is wide and stretches from 48th Street near the Tempe-Phoenix border to almost 51st Avenue in Laveen. The preserve is bordered by the villages of Laveen, Ahwatukee, South Mountain, and Ahwatukee Foothills and spans about 12 miles.

The park was originally part of Franklin D. Roosevelt's plan to put America back to work. During the Depression, men of the Civilian Conservation Corps built more than 40 miles of hiking trails, buildings, and firepits. Additional miles of hiking trails have been added since then, and more than 50 miles of trails, many of them

---

The Phoenix bedroom community Ahwatukee is located along the south side of the preserve.

SOUTH MOUNTAIN PARK PRESERVE

WHAT One of the largest city parks in the United States

WHERE 10919 S. Central Ave., Phoenix, Arizona

COST Free

PRO TIP Drive to Dobbins Lookout by Summit Road off Central Avenue for a view of the Phoenix skyline.

Top: The golf course at Arizona Grand borders the South Mountain Park Preserve. Above: The view of South Mountain from Baseline Road in south Phoenix.

open to mountain bikers and horses as well as hikers, are available. In spring, winter, and fall, parking can get crowded, but once on the trails the crowds tend to disperse over the thousands of acres. The eastern edge of the park shares a border with the Arizona Grand Resort and its golf course. The line where manicured golf course and wild desert meet is clearly visible from the Beverly Canyon Trail. Other popular trails include Holbert Trail, which leads to Dobbins Lookout and is accessible from Central Avenue and Dobbins, and Telegraph Pass Trail, which you can access from Desert Foothills Parkway on the south side of the preserve.

FRANK'S HIDDEN TREASURES

Is that a Frank Lloyd Wright house?

It might be. Several Frank Lloyd Wright-designed and -inspired homes and buildings can be found in and around the Phoenix area. Among them are the Arizona Biltmore Resort, Gammage Auditorium, the Harold Price House in Paradise Valley, and the First Christian Church in Phoenix, not to mention his jewel of the west—Taliesin West. Not all of these homes and buildings are open for tours, and not all of them were officially designed by Wright. Architect Albert Chase McArthur designed the Arizona Biltmore but with consultative input from Wright, who was his mentor. In fact, some say that the only building Wright officially designed on commission in Arizona is Arizona State University's Gammage Auditorium in Tempe. He did, however, inspire other architects, offer consultative help, and draw designs that were later modified and used after his death, including one for the First Christian Church in north Phoenix. He also designed several homes throughout the Valley. One home in particular has recently raised local awareness. The David Wright House, designed by Frank Lloyd Wright for his son David and David's wife, Gladys, was almost demolished in the early 2010s. Located in the much sought-after Arcadia neighborhood in the shadows of Camelback Mountain,

---

Wright's design for Gammage Auditorium was originally meant for an opera house in Baghdad, Iraq.

Gammage Auditorium in Tempe at Mill Avenue and Apache Boulevard.

the owners at the time, affected by the recession of 2008, were forced to sell to developers, who, failing to recognize the significance of the property, had planned to tear down the structure and put two homes in its place. Public outcry and petitions put a halt to the project, and in 2012 another buyer purchased the property and presented it to the David and Gladys Wright Foundation. It is currently being renovated and preserved.

GAMMAGE AUDITORIUM

WHAT A Frank Lloyd Wright building

WHERE 1200 S. Forest Ave., Tempe, Arizona

COST Free (or the cost of a ticket)

PRO TIP Taliesin West offers tours, programs and events.

8 HISTORIC MOTEL TAKES A BATH

What will happen to Buckhorn Baths? But, wait, what is it?

Much has been written about Buckhorn Baths, especially in the last several years since the property closed and the City of Mesa failed to purchase it from the jaws of inevitable destruction. While efforts have been made to preserve the historic property, also known as Buckhorn Mineral Wells, no one has been able to pull it off. When owner Ted Sliger began drilling a well sometime in the late 1930s on a plot of land about seven miles from Mesa, he discovered something quite unexpected—a natural hot spring in the middle of the desert. He and his wife, Alice, soon used the hot spring to open their mineral baths in 1939. Their business prospered for more than 60 years, especially since the baths were a favored destination for the professional Cactus League ballplayers and their coaches and owners who visited every spring. An advertisement from 1942 boasted of modern cottages and a modern bathhouse with separate bathrooms for what they called "patients." Today, the big neon sign, motel façade, and tiny adobe-brick cabins can be seen fading into the past at the northwest corner of Recker Road and Main Street. A big, red "For Sale" sign stands at the corner as well.

BUCKHORN BATHS MOTEL

WHAT A historic mineral well and motel

WHERE 5984 E. Main St., Mesa, Arizona

COST Free

PRO TIP For now, the cottages and main building and neon sign are there to see.

Above: The historic cottages at Buckhorn Baths.
Left: A "For Sale" sign stands in front of the old neon Buckhorn Baths sign on Main Street in Mesa.

The Buckhorn Baths' neon sign was created by the Mesa-based Guerrero Lindsey Sign Company.

9 LEGEND OF THE LOST DUTCHMAN'S GOLD

Is there really gold hidden in the Superstition Mountains?

The Lost Dutchman's gold may very well be Arizona's most famous story of hidden treasure. While most locals assume the story is simply a tall tale, more than a few researchers and treasure hunters from around the world have trekked into the Superstitions in search of what is said to be millions of dollars' worth of gold. The story begins with the Spanish explorer Coronado, who scoured the region in the 1540s in search of the seven golden cities. While local Indians confirmed the existence of gold in the area, Coronado and his men fled before they could find it—victims of a series of mysterious disappearances and disturbing murders. It wasn't until almost 300 years later that Don Miguel Peralta from Sonora, Mexico, found the elusive gold. For the next three years, he and his men worked the mine, sending the gold south into Mexico, but Apache Indians decided to retaliate. As Peralta and his men attempted to flee the area, the Apaches attacked. They scattered men, mules, and money across the area, which later became known as Gold Field. In the decades that followed, the occasional

THE LEGEND OF THE LOST DUTCHMAN'S GOLD

WHAT A tale of lost treasure

WHERE Superstition Mountains.

COST Free

PRO TIP For a few dollars, you can hear the legend of the Lost Dutchman's Gold on the train ride at Goldfield Ghost Town, the site of the old mining town, near Apache Junction.

20

explorer or prospector came upon some of these remains, often finding saddlebags filled with gold ore.

After the attack on Peralta, many sought the mine, but the most well-known treasure seeker is Jacob Waltz (or Walz as some stories go). Legend has it that Waltz discovered the mine, but whether he did it on his own or with the help of Don Miguel Peralta (whose life he is said to have saved) is not clear. Regardless, stories agree that Waltz and his mining partner, Jacob Weiser, mined the vein, because witnesses claimed the two men spent the next two decades purchasing goods in Phoenix with some of the purest gold ore Phoenicians had ever seen. Somewhere along the way, Weiser disappeared. Some say Waltz killed him to keep the mine a secret, but his was not the only death, and many attributed other mysterious deaths and disappearances to Waltz, the Apaches, and even to the Superstitions, which are aptly named and considered very dangerous. In 1891, Waltz died, and with his death the secret of the mine was lost, thus making it "The Lost Dutchman's Mine."

The location of the "Lost Dutchman's Gold" is a secret that has yet to be revealed, but that doesn't keep treasure seekers from looking. For more than a century and a quarter, prospectors, explorers, and even hikers have trekked into the Superstitions looking for the gold. Some have never returned.

Jacob Waltz was German, not Dutch. Many believe he received his moniker because he was considered "the Deutsch man"; over time he became known as the Dutchman. The Town of Apache Junction hosts a three-day Lost Dutchman Days every spring.

MOVIES THE WAY THEY WERE MEANT TO BE

Can I still see performances at the old Orpheum Theatre?

When the Orpheum Theatre opened in 1929, it was the belle of a ball already filled with beautiful ladies. Funded by Rickards and Nace Amusement Enterprises, Inc., it would be one of several such theaters in the downtown Phoenix area and across the country, but the two men insisted on the best of everything. From the intricately carved arches framing the stage to the state-of-the-art acoustical construction and sound system, the men set out to create the finest theater in the West. Neon tubing lit up the tower and the grand marquee, beckoning evening guests from its place on the southeast corner of Adams Street and 2nd Avenue. The building's interior and exterior design exhibited Spanish, Italian, and Moorish influences, and the Spanish doñas (or ladies) placed at intervals along the exterior exemplified the state's early Spanish influence. The interior, complete with hardwood floors, rich carpeting, and antique beams, created a luxurious experience for showgoers. When it opened, the *Arizona Republic* called it one of the finest show houses west of the Mississippi. In its day, the Orpheum was designed to play the latest "talkies" coming out of

It took 12 years and $14 million to restore the Orpheum to its earliest version.

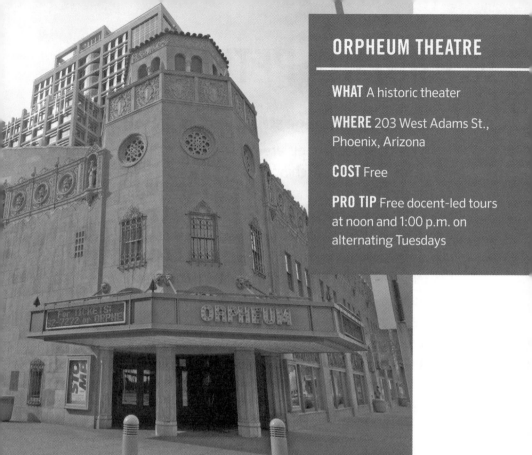

The Orpheum Theatre at Cesar Chavez Memorial Plaza; Phoenix City Hall towers in the background.

Hollywood, but the building bears no resemblance to the movie theaters of the 21st century. Today, it is the last theater of its kind in the Valley. After passing through a series of hands (and names), including Paramount Pictures, the beautiful Orpheum Theatre was all but abandoned until the City of Phoenix purchased it from the Corona Family in 1984 and began restoring it. Today, while you can no longer watch movies at the Orpheum, you can watch an off-Broadway play or national comedy or musical act and catch a glimpse of what moviegoing once was.

PHOENIX PETROGLYPHS

What are those strange scribblings on the rocks?

Those strange symbols are not modern graffiti. Instead, they are mysterious etchings made by several civilizations across the millennia. The ancient Hohokam who lived along the river banks left behind more than their canals. They also left behind countless rock carvings that you can see along hiking trails in the South Mountain Park Preserve in South Phoenix, but these are not the only petroglyphs in the Phoenix area and not the oldest. Farther north and west is the Deer Valley Petroglyph Preserve (formerly known as the Deer Valley Rock Art Center), which showcases a series of drawings, including those from the Hohokam as well as those carved by older Native American civilizations scrawled across more than 500 boulders and spanning more than 10,000 years. The center is now part of Arizona State University and includes the 47-acre preserve and an archeology museum. The carvings include symbols and signs as well as images of animals and hunters. The art tells the story of an ancient people that farmed and hunted across the area long before the pioneers arrived.

Skunk Creek passes through the Deer Valley Petroglyph Preserve.

The entrance to the Deer Valley Petroglyph Preserve in the West Valley.

PETROGLYPHS

WHAT Ancient rock art

WHERE South Mountain Park Preserve and Deer Valley Petroglyph Preserve

COST South Mountain Park (Free); Deer Valley ($3-$7 per person)

PRO TIP The petroglyphs are a delightful surprise to hikers along the South Mountain trails, but for a sure sighting, visit the Deer Valley Preserve.

<u>12</u> #1 CITY FOR PIZZA

Really? Phoenix has the best pizza?

When you think of world-class pizza and number one cities for ooey-gooey, cheesy pies, Phoenix isn't necessarily the first city to come to mind. New York City and Chicago, sure, but not Phoenix. While that may be true, to quote Bob Dylan, "The times they are a-changin'." In 2016, readers of *Travel + Leisure* magazine picked a few new leaders (in fact, NYC and Chicago didn't even make the top three), and Phoenix ended up in the top spot. Maybe it's all those New Yorkers and Chicagoans flooding the city in droves—some as seasonal snowbirds and others as full-time residents—demanding top-notch pizza. Or maybe it's simply that Chris Bianco, the number one pizza maker and internationally acclaimed chef of the Southwest, decided to build his pizza-making empire right here in Phoenix. Whatever the reason, Phoenix apparently has fantastic pizza. This could be why Chicago strongholds and such pizza kings as Giordano's, Gino's East, and Lou Malnati's have all trekked out to the desert in the last couple of years to expand their chains and spread their own blends of crispy dough, gooey cheese, and tasty

---

Several different kinds of pizza are available here in Phoenix, including Chicago-style deep dish and thin crust, NY-style medium crust, and brick-oven fired and artisan pies.

Pizzeria Bianco's original location can be found in downtown Phoenix at Arizona Heritage & Science Park.

toppings west. These Chicago giants, however, have their work cut out for them. Phoenix is now second to none, and as the already-established home of such local favorites as Pizzeria Bianco, Oregano's, Cibo Urban Pizzeria, and Spinato's, a couple of other pizza places are already on top.

PHOENIX VOTED #1 CITY FOR PIZZA

WHAT A pizza legend

WHERE Any number of local pizza joints.

COST Varies

PRO TIP Pizzeria Bianco's downtown often has long wait times. Try their location at Town & Country in the Phoenix Biltmore neighborhood instead.

<u>13</u> ST. MARY'S BASILICA

Did a saint visit St. Mary's Basilica in Phoenix?

When Pope John Paul II visited St. Mary's Basilica in 1987, he wasn't yet a saint. That honor bestowed by the Catholic Church would not come until 2014, long after his death, but a man who would be saint did visit St. Mary's. During his tour of the United States, Pope John Paul II visited Phoenix and spoke to a crowd of thousands from the balcony of the church. In 1985, he had named the Church of the Immaculate Conception of the Blessed Virgin Mary (St. Mary's official name) a minor basilica. The term "basilica" has both canonical and architectural significance. Canonically, it is a special designation given by the Catholic Pope to a church, bestowing upon it specific rights and privileges. It was the 32nd minor basilica to be named in the United States and the only basilica in Arizona. Less than 100 such designated churches are located in the United States, and St. Mary's is one of about 10 in the Western United States.

Located in downtown Phoenix, St. Mary's Basilica is the second-oldest church in Phoenix. Built in 1915, its unique structure takes up an entire city block. In the early days of Phoenix, it was considered the tallest structure in the downtown area. Today, you can still hear the bell tolling on the hour. For $2.00, you can grab one of the tour pamphlets from the gift shop on Monroe.

ST. MARY'S BASILICA

WHAT A historic church

WHERE 231 N. 3rd St., Phoenix, Arizona

COST $2.00 for the tour pamphlet

PRO TIP The pamphlet guides guests through a tour of the property.

Top: St. Mary's Basilica, an impressive structure among the city's skyscrapers.
Above: The entrance to the Via Assisi Gift Shop on Monroe Street.

The basement portion of the church,
now the social hall, was
finished in 1903.

14 TEMPE'S OLD PUEBLO

Is that an old pueblo?

The historic Eisendrath House looks more like a home in Santa Fe than one in Tempe. When the Jewish heiress and widow Rose Eisendrath found herself shunned from some of the premier resorts in Scottsdale, she commissioned architect Robert T. Evans to create one for her. Not to be left out of the Hollywood circle of stars that frequented the Scottsdale area, Eisendrath bankrolled a resort-worthy home. The stunning 5,250-square-foot adobe-style home is reminiscent of an old pueblo and stands high on a hill in an area of Papago Park called Elfin Hills. Eisendrath originally furnished her home with a combination of Queen Anne and Early American furniture with Indian rug accents. The home has a hidden courtyard, a wide front balcony, and the traditional wooden beams of pueblo-style architecture. It is considered by the City of Tempe to be the oldest example of Pueblo Revival architecture in town. Until her death in 1936, the Eisendrath House served as a winter resort for the wealthy. Today, after quite a bit of money and time spent on renovations, it towers regally above Arizona Heritage Center and serves as both the city's center for water conservation and an event space.

On clear days, the front balcony offers a panoramic view of the surrounding mountains.

The Pueblo Revival home stands out against the desert sky.

THE EISENDRATH CENTER FOR WATER CONVERSATION

WHAT A historic event center

WHERE 1400 N. College Dr., Tempe, Arizona

COST Free

PRO TIP Docent-led tours are available by appointment Thursdays and Saturdays; call 480-473-0245.

15 THE OLDEST HOME IN PHOENIX

What is that odd-looking building on Buckeye Road?

The Jones-Montoya House, built in 1879 by the Anglo-Mexican couple Dr. Wilson Walker Jones and Alcaria Montoya, may not seem old by East Coast standards, but it is the oldest documented home still standing in Phoenix. The 19th-century adobe building sits back from Buckeye Road just east of the downtown Phoenix area. It has occasionally been confused with the odd-looking structure made of rocks that you see along Buckeye Road. This structure stands out against the commercial plaza that went up several years ago. It was once brown and sagging and surrounded by a tall iron fence; in recent years, it has been painted white and beautifully landscaped, but it is not the Jones-Montoya House. That is set farther back on the property. Once the homestead for the family farm, the Jones-Montoyas raised their seven children there. Over the decades, efforts have been made to preserve the home, including the rotting wooden porch (probably used as a sleeping porch on hot summer nights). The windows and doors have been boarded up, and a construction fence, complete with green, plastic sheeting, surrounds the structure. Since the local nonprofit Chicanos Por La

Today, the Jones-Montoya Home remains a testament to the building practices of old Phoenix—sun-dried bricks made of mud, hay, and water.

32

Watch for this white-painted stone structure that was once an old produce stand. It serves as a marker for the Jones-Montoya House.

Causa bought the home several years ago, many people have hoped that the structure will be restored and opened for use. As for the odd-looking building fronting Buckeye Road, that is actually an old produce stand.

THE JONES-MONTOYA HOUSE

WHAT The oldest documented home in Phoenix

WHERE 1008 E. Buckeye Rd., Phoenix

COST Free

PRO TIP The Jones-Montoya house is set farther back from the street.

THE STEALTHY PHILANTHROPIST

Who is Virginia G. Piper?

Locals have probably noticed the name Virginia G. Piper popping up all over the Valley over the last decade or two. But many people don't know who she is. Her name can be found at Symphony Hall, on ASU's campus, and sprinkled across hospitals, schools, and numerous arts and cultural organizations around Maricopa County. What you may not know is that Virginia G. Piper was once the wife of Motorola founder Paul V. Galvin. They met in Illinois and married in 1945. Over their 14-year marriage, they regularly traveled to Paradise Valley so that Galvin could visit the Motorola site in Phoenix. Paul taught Virginia how to navigate the social strata he had attained and guided her in the art of philanthropic giving. Upon his death in 1959, Virginia carried on his work, administering his charitable trust in Chicago. She didn't marry her second husband, Kenneth Piper (a vice president at Motorola, Inc., in Illinois), until 1969, and they moved to Arizona permanently in 1972. Ken died only three years later. For the next 25 years, Virginia fully dedicated herself to philanthropic efforts—chairing events, supporting individuals and organizations, and giving her time, treasure, and talents to the county of Maricopa. She died in 1999, and per her will established the $600 million Virginia G. Piper

Galvin Parkway, which bisects Papago Park, is named after Paul V. Galvin. It was dedicated in the 1960s.

One of many local entities funded by the Virginia G. Piper Trust.

Charitable Trust. Since 2000, the trust has donated more than $370 million to local organizations and charities, giving an average of $25 million annually.

Several other similarly endowed trusts and generous families and individuals have over the years increased awareness of and access to arts, culture, medicine, education, and religion in the Valley, including the Nina Mason Pulliam Charitable Trust, which funded the Audubon Center in south Phoenix, and philanthropists Katherine and Robert Herberger (for whom the Herberger Theater Center is named).

17 THE SECRET ROOM AT FOUR PEAKS BREWERY

What's behind door number two?

No. It's not the giant safe you want to sneak a peek at. It's the nondescript door to the right that houses what many consider Alternative Rock gold. What is now a tiny maintenance closet in the recently refurbished tasting room at Four Peaks Brewery in Tempe was once the even tinier bathroom in the Gin Blossoms' old recording studio. Over the past twenty-something years, Uranus Recording, owned by Gin Blossom Robin Wilson, has recorded such superstars as Phoenix-born Stevie Nicks of Fleetwood Mac; local legend Roger Clyne; folk-rock bands, such as the Nitty Gritty Dirt Band; and rising star Ed Sheeran. Over the years, some of these recording artists have left behind mementos—signatures, band names, thank-you notes, smart comments, and even sketches and drawings. Scrawled across the walls, the door, and even the ceiling are such names as the Velvet Ants, such comments as "long live the Pistoleros," and signatures from the likes of Kris Roe of punk rock band the Ataris. When Robin Wilson decided to close the studio in 2015, the owners at Four Peaks agreed to take over the space.

The homegrown Tempe band Gin Blossoms started in 1987, achieved multiplatinum success, and is still recording after a brief hiatus.

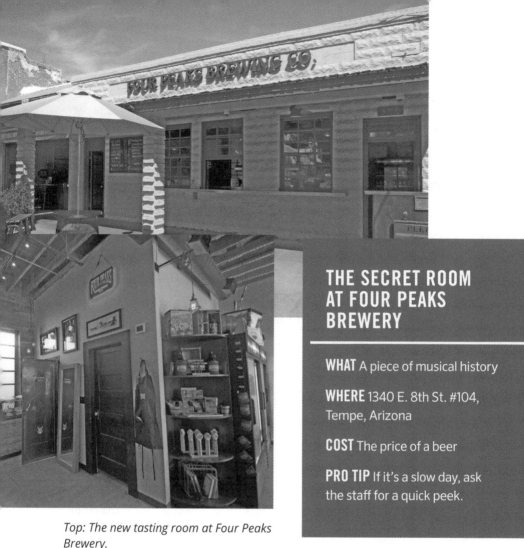

THE SECRET ROOM AT FOUR PEAKS BREWERY

WHAT A piece of musical history

WHERE 1340 E. 8th St. #104, Tempe, Arizona

COST The price of a beer

PRO TIP If it's a slow day, ask the staff for a quick peek.

Top: The new tasting room at Four Peaks Brewery.
Above: The door to the Secret Room.

Later that same year Four Peaks Brewery partnered with international powerhouse Anheuser-Busch to take their beer beyond Arizona's borders, gaining their own kind of multiplatinum success. The next year Four Peaks reopened the studio as their tasting room. They had uncovered the windows, finished the floors, added a bar, and exposed the building's framework. In the process, they preserved another important part of Tempe history. Today, you can experience two homegrown success stories in one location.

18 YOU HAVE THE RIGHT TO REMAIN SILENT

What's the connection between Arizona and the Miranda Warning?

Since it became a territory in 1863, Arizona has had its fair share of infamous criminals. Ernesto Arturo Miranda may be the most well known. His notoriety is less about the crime he was charged with and more about the ripple effect his case made when it went to the highest court in the land. In 1963, when Miranda was arrested by the Phoenix Police Department, they took him back to the City-County Building but failed to advise him of his right to have an attorney present. That simple fact snowballed into a landmark decision by the U.S. Supreme Court in 1966. You may have heard the 40-word statement that resulted from Miranda's time in the legal limelight. This handful of sentences has been immortalized by cop shows on TV and in the movies. They begin with the following words: "You have the right to remain silent..." The criminal justice system has Miranda to thank for that. In fact, his very name has become a verb—when an officer reads the Miranda warning to a suspect, that suspect has been mirandized.

The City-County Building, known today as the Maricopa County Courthouse, also housed the Phoenix Police Department from 1928 to 1975.

Top: The Phoenix Police Department Museum is located at Cesar Chavez Plaza.

Inset: The City of Mesa Cemetery where Ernesto Miranda is buried.

Miranda ended up serving time for the crime after a jury convicted him in a retrial. About four years after he was released from jail, he was killed in a knife fight in a bar in Phoenix. Today, Miranda is resting peacefully in the City of Mesa Cemetery. You can learn about this and other well-known criminal history stories at the Phoenix Police Department Museum, located in the very same building where Miranda was once incorrectly interviewed.

THE MIRANDA WARNING

WHAT A bit of criminal justice history

WHERE E. Jefferson St., Phoenix, Arizona

COST Free; donations accepted

PRO TIP The building's topmost tier was once the city jail.

A DIRECTOR'S DEBUT

Where did Steven Spielberg make his first movie debut?

A good 30 years or so before the Phoenix Lights awed thousands of Phoenicians, Steven Spielberg debuted his first movie, *Firelight*, at the tender age of 16. Spielberg was intrigued early on by the thought of extraterrestrial life. His father often dragged him and his three siblings out into the Phoenix desert to watch the stars, comets, and meteor showers that were so vivid away from the bright lights of a big city. *Firelight* debuted in 1963 at the Phoenix Little Theatre and was the precursor to Spielberg's big break in 1977, *Close Encounters of the Third Kind*.

Spielberg lived in Phoenix during his formative years and went to Arcadia High School. He's not the only famous person to grow up in Phoenix. Other big acts include actor Nick Nolte (who also had his debut at the Phoenix Little Theatre in *The Rose Tattoo* in 1968), rocker Alice Cooper, singer Stevie Nicks, *American Idol* winner Jordin Sparks, and actress Emma Stone—to name a few.

In 2013, Spielberg returned to Phoenix and cohosted an event for the Phoenix Symphony with award-winning composer and collaborator John Williams, who composed the music for some of Spielberg's biggest films.

Spielberg attended Arcadia High School along with Lynda Carter of Wonder Woman fame.

PHOENIX THEATRE

WHAT A historic theater

WHERE 100 E. McDowell Rd., Phoenix, Arizona

COST The price of a show

Top: Phoenix Theatre adjacent to the Phoenix Art Museum.
Above: Steven Spielberg depicted in the wall mural at First Studio.

THE LEGEND OF THE LOST CAMELS

Are camels still wandering around in Arizona?

For years rumors circulated about camels wandering the Arizona desert. Some claimed they were real live camels, while others insisted they were camel apparitions with skeletons upon their backs. Real or imagined, camels were once in Arizona courtesy of the U.S. military. Two men, one nicknamed Greek George and the other Hi Jolly, taught the soldiers how to work with the camels. The animals were an exotic treat to everyone who saw them, but their time in the United States Camel Military Corps didn't last too long. The Civil War eventually usurped money and attention, and the camels were sold or escaped, hence the rumor that wild camels were afoot in Arizona.

Today, the only wild camel in Phoenix is the one lying on its side just north of Camelback Road. Camelback Mountain, aptly named for its surprising likeness to a reclining camel (head and hump), is one of the most iconic mountains in Phoenix. Seen from all points across the Valley, it's a visual landmark that immediately orients both newcomers and longtime residents. One of the most beautiful mountains, especially as the sun sets in the city, it is also the highest summit in the Valley at

Camelback Mountain has two trails, both difficult: Echo Canyon and Cholla Trail.

Camelback Mountain, the only "wild" camel left in Arizona.

just over 2,700 feet. Located in the heart of the Biltmore District, several of the city's most prestigious resorts, including Royal Palms Resort, The Phoenician, Camelback Sanctuary, and Camelback Inn, command stunning views of the mountainside.

CAMELBACK MOUNTAIN

WHAT An iconic mountain

WHERE Off Camelback Road

COST Free

PRO TIP Echo Canyon is often so packed you'll see a line of cars waiting to park; go early.

21 CHANDLER'S OSTRICH OBSESSION

Where can I find an ostrich?

Ostrich ranching is a unique piece of the City of Chandler's history, and in recent years the city and chamber of commerce have found a way to celebrate its kind of peculiar history. First brought to the United States toward the end of the 19th century, ostriches were largely raised for their contribution to women's fashion in the early part of the 20th century.

Dr. A. J. Chandler, founder of Chandler and the San Marcos Resort, was fascinated by the animals when he first encountered them at the Chicago World's Fair in 1893. In 1905, he became one the first ranchers to import them into Arizona and begin raising them. Chandler was convinced that the animal's feathers would be the height of women's fashion for years to come. Inspired by his vision, others began raising the odd-looking birds. Thus, Chandler's ostrich obsession became the impetus for the ostrich craze you see today in Chandler. You'll usually see the colorful ostrich Cee Cee standing outside of Sibley's West in downtown Chandler, and city hall sometimes has one on display, usually to promote the annual Ostrich Festival.

CHANDLER'S OSTRICH FESTIVAL

WHAT A festival

WHERE 745 E. Germann Rd., Chandler, Arizona

COST $7–10 per ticket

PRO TIP The three-day weekend event typically takes place in early March.

44

This beautiful ostrich can often be found standing around downtown Chandler—pictured here at city hall.

Another one can be found in the underground speakeasy The Ostrich below Crust at the San Marcos. In celebration of the city's founder and its ostrich heritage, the Chandler Chamber of Commerce has hosted the annual festival at Tumbleweed Park since 1989.

The Ostrich Festival was featured in the 1995 movie *Waiting to Exhale*. The novel, written by Terry McMillan, is set in Phoenix, Arizona.

22 ARIZONA'S HOT DOG TRADITION

What is a Sonoran Dog, and where can I find one?

The Sonoran Dog is not the kind of canine that barks. Instead, this dog is a hot dog, and the Sonoran Dog is Arizona's interpretation of another American favorite. Adding a dash of Southwest to the traditional dog, local hot dog lovers decided that instead of the traditional onions, relish, pickles, and mustard, these puppies should be wrapped in bacon, covered in beans, sprinkled with cheese, and layered with sauteed onions, a few jalapeños, and a little mustard for good measure. Sometimes it's served in a bun, and at other times it's nestled in naan and named a Moki, as it is at Short Leash Hotdogs. The variations depend on the restaurant (or food truck) you frequent, but the Sonoran Dog comes with a decidedly Southwestern spin, and the components are usually a riff on the basic ingredients—beans, tomatoes, bacon, jalapeño, cheese, onions, and mayo. The Best Dressed Dog (a food truck) adds bacon jam, and El Güero Canelo in the West Valley uses a jalapeño sauce. The Sonoran Dog at The Lodge Sasquatch Kitchen in Tempe may be a hidden gem. Tucked among the lines of an already

Even Adam Richman of the Travel Channel's Man vs. Food favored El Güero Canelo's Sonoran Dog in a 2010 episode of the show.

46

Top: A beer and a Sonoran Dog.
Inset: The Sonoran Dog piled high with cojita cheese and jalapeños.

packed menu, this dog is downright delicious—wrapped in bacon and piled high with pinto beans, cojita cheese, mayo and mustard, and fresh, sliced jalapeños. The Sonoran Dog is so hot that it may give local favorites Ted's Hot Dogs and Portillo's (a Chicago chain) a little competition.

SONORAN DOG

WHAT An Arizona tradition

WHERE Numerous restaurants throughout the Valley

COST $3–$8+ depending on the restaurant

PRO TIP Pair the Papago Orange Blossom with a Sonoran Dog at The Lodge in Tempe.

23 A HIDDEN OASIS AT ASU

Is there a Secret Garden on ASU's Tempe campus?

The Secret Garden isn't so secret anymore. Google "ASU and secret garden" and you'll find the address and map right there on your screen. The directions are still a bit vague, but check out one of those aerial views and you'll see it. Gaining access to it, however, may be another story. You can walk right past it and never know what's hiding on the other side of those old buildings. Students taking classes in nearby halls have certainly heard the rumors, but unless they were looking for it (or in a room looking out on it), they probably didn't run across it on their own. It's not quite as hidden perhaps as the Lost Dutchman's Mine, but it's still a little bit of a treasure hunt.

The garden is situated between what were once two student dormitories, one of which was an all-girls dorm. The entrance for one of the halls is directly across from the lawn above Hayden Library. The other opens onto Forest Mall. Without giving it all away, one of those entryways has a doorbell beside the front door. You can access the garden through the buildings surrounding it and through an external passageway that will lead you directly into the garden, but it's up to you to find it.

Once inside either building, you will need to navigate the hallways to find one of the exterior doors leading to the secret garden.

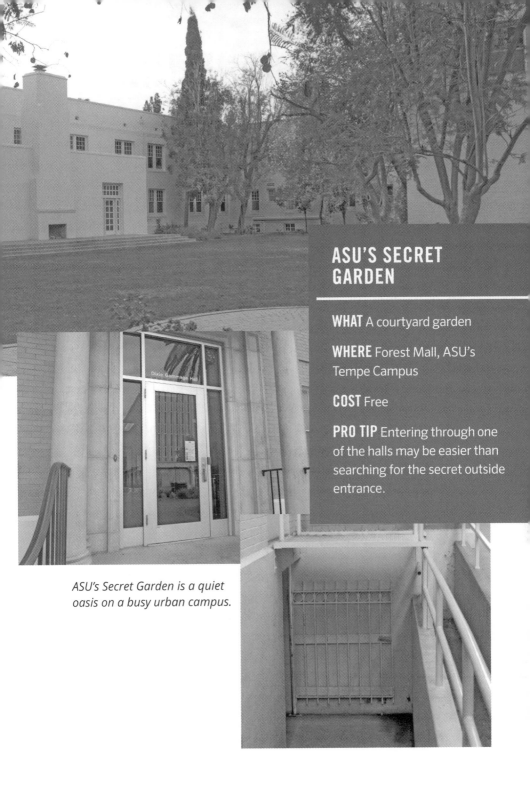

ASU'S SECRET GARDEN

WHAT A courtyard garden

WHERE Forest Mall, ASU's Tempe Campus

COST Free

PRO TIP Entering through one of the halls may be easier than searching for the secret outside entrance.

ASU's Secret Garden is a quiet oasis on a busy urban campus.

24 BUILT TO STAND THE TEST OF TIME

What is the giant temple in downtown Mesa?

The City of Mesa was originally settled by Mormon pioneers in 1878 as they traveled south into Arizona. In 1927, the congregation built the massive temple to serve the local Mormon community. The temple took about five years to build, and when it opened its doors it was the first temple of its kind in Arizona. The builders designed the 114,000-square-foot concrete structure to last, creating four-foot-thick walls and reinforcing them with 127 tons of steel.

Today, it is considered the seventh operating temple of the Church of the Latter-day Saints. Located downtown, it strikes an imposing silhouette in the heart of Mesa. The 20-acre property faces Pioneer Park to the north. Every spring the wide front lawn on Main Street is covered with a stage and folding chairs for the largest outdoor Easter Pageant in the world. The temple has served as a house of worship for the local Mormon community for almost a century. The building is covered in terra-cotta tiles, and Biblical stories are carved into each of the temple's four corners. One of its hidden charms is the beautiful flower garden and reflecting pool. The building fronting Main Street is the Visitors' Center. Slip past the wide-open iron gates beyond the center for a peek

The Mesa Arizona Temple and reflecting pool.

Top: Chairs set up in anticipation for the annual outdoor Easter pageant (the largest in the world).
Right: The temple is surrounded by a beautifully maintained garden.

at the carefully manicured grounds.

At Christmastime, the property is decorated with hundreds of thousands of lights and can be seen for blocks around. The annual nondenominational display first appeared in 1980 and was named "one of the three must-see displays in the U.S." by *Good Morning America*.

MESA ARIZONA TEMPLE

WHAT A Mormon Temple

WHERE 101 S. LeSueur, Mesa, Arizona

COST Free

PRO TIP The Visitors' Center fronts Main Street. For a view of the Temple, follow the footpath beyond the center to the temple, garden, and reflecting pool.

The Mormon community designed the building to withstand the sands of time; all that concrete and steel is meant to last another 30,000 years.

25 THE UNFINISHED PHOENIX FINANCIAL CENTER

Hanging chads, anyone?

If the Phoenix Financial Center looks a little lopsided, it is. The second tower, which would have stood above the north rotunda on Mitchell Drive, was never built. When St. Louis-based architect W. A. Sarmiento designed the eight-acre complex in the early 1960s for David H. Murdoch, president of the Financial Corporation of Arizona, no one anticipated that the economy might have other plans. In 1964, the first phase of the project was completed: a 10-story south tower and two matching rotundas. The second phase: the addition of nine stories (originally expected to be only eight) to the south tower was completed in 1972. But the final piece—a matching north tower high-rise—was never added. Today, locals unceremoniously refer to the south tower as the "Punchcard Building." While it does resemble an old computer punch card, Sarmiento denied he meant it to look like one. Sarmiento also designed the Western Savings & Loan's West Valley branch at Metro Center in 1975. It is now a Souper! Salad! restaurant and is clearly visible from Interstate 17.

If you take a look at the Phoenix Financial Center using Google Maps, you'll clearly see what has been left undone.

The South Tower of the Phoenix Financial Center faces Osborn Avenue.

The South Rotunda building was restored and renovated by the Boston- and Phoenix-based architecture firm Shepley Bulfinch in 2014. It now serves as their office and design studio.

PHOENIX FINANCIAL CENTER

WHAT A missing piece of skyline

WHERE 3443 N. Central Ave., Phoenix, Arizona

COST Free

PHOENIX'S HIDDEN AMUSEMENT PARK

Where can I find Enchanted Island?

This enchanted island, reminiscent of Coney Island's carnival atmosphere, is hidden deep inside Encanto Park in the historic Encanto neighborhood of central Phoenix. The nearly eight-acre amusement park was originally named KiddieLand when it opened in 1946. For 40 years, it entertained Phoenix children until it closed for renovations in 1986. The City of Phoenix opened it again in 1991 and renamed it Enchanted Island Amusement Park. The concrete bridge leads children of all ages from the parking

Enchanted Island Amusement Park at Encanto Park.

lot at Encanto Park into the cool shade of the amusement park. Grab a bag of salty popcorn and a frozen ice cream bar, and wait your turn for a ride on the little train that loops through the park or for a seat on one of the carved horses on the historic Allan Herschell carousel. Or, better yet, on a warm spring day, take a ride on one of the pedal boats around the Encanto Lagoon.

Encanto Park is 222 acres of lush green grass, towering palms, waterways, and a lagoon,

Encanto Park was named one of Forbes magazine's Best City Parks in America.

Top: Enchanted Island
Amusement Park at Encanto Park.
Above: One of the many bridges
at Encanto Park.

ENCHANTED ISLAND

WHAT An amusement park

WHERE 1202 W. Encanto Blvd.,
Phoenix, Arizona

COST Admission is free; tickets
required for the rides ($1.50/
ticket)

PRO TIP Spring and fall are a
perfect time to visit.

all in the middle of a bustling
metropolis. Dotted with islands,
two golf courses, a driving
range, putting green, trails,
fishing spots, and at least one
local weekend yoga group, it's a
peaceful little oasis.

<u>27</u> STRAIGHT ON 'TIL SUN CITY

Why is Grand Avenue at an angle?

Grand Avenue, which originates at the intersection of Van Buren and 7th Avenue just west of downtown Phoenix, is an anomaly. Running counter to the gridlike street pattern of Phoenix, the diagonal line it cuts across the west side was intentional. When early developers began buying land north and west of the original Phoenix townsite, they wanted an

Street art decorates Grand Avenue as it passes through the Grand Avenue Arts District.

easy way for folks to get back and forth between these new developments and the city's center. The plan worked for several decades before Grand Avenue, also known as the Phoenix-Wickenburg Highway, was bypassed in the late 1970s when Interstate 10 was finished. The new interstate circumvented the historic strip and the 1940s- and '50s-era buildings soon fell into disrepair. Today, Grand Avenue has quite a bit more to offer than a direct path to Sun City. Since

Since 2008, the Grand Avenue Arts & Preservation group has hosted an annual Grand Avenue Festival in November.

Top: *Chartreuse Gallery now occupies the historic Bragg's Pie Factory on Grand Avenue.*
Inset: *Bikes for rent and the designated bike path along Grand Avenue encourage biking through the arts district.*

GRAND AVENUE

WHAT An arts & entertainment district

WHERE McDowell Road south to Van Buren Street; Seventh Avenue west to 19th Avenue

COST Free

PRO TIP Grab lunch or dinner at internationally acclaimed Chef Silvana Salcido Esparza's Barrio Café Gran Reserva at the corner of Grand Avenue and McKinley Street.

the early 2000s, residents and businesses have made a comeback. Fueled by the local arts community, including many Hispanic, Chicano, and Latino artists, efforts have been made to preserve the history of the area and revitalize the storefronts, warehouses, and structures along both sides of the avenue. What was once a dilapidated and forgotten thoroughfare is now taking on a life of its own. More than 20 murals by local artists cover the buildings, primarily clustered around what locals call the Six Points, where Grand Avenue intersects 15th Avenue and Roosevelt Street in the heart of the community. The area is filling up with coffee shops, art galleries, studios, restaurants, and bars.

28 ARIZONA'S COPPER DOME

What is that shining beacon atop the capitol building?

Surprisingly, the copper dome mentioned above does not refer to any type of sports arena; it does, however, point to another type of arena—this time a political one. This shining dome of copper crowns the state capitol building and sits 95 feet above the desert floor. The dome was originally made of zinc and steel when the building was added in 1901. Eleven years before Arizona became a state, it was the City of Phoenix's tribute to its new status as the territorial capital. Designed to represent one of the state's five original economic pillars (copper), the dome gained its shiny-penny look in 1978. It was repaired after a massive hailstorm in late 2011 just in time for the state's centennial celebration in 2012. The Winged Victory atop the copper dome is a 600-pound, 17-foot weather vane. Rumor has it that when workers climbed to the top of the dome to repair the goddess after a weather-related injury, they found bullet holes in her wings. Apparently, the cowboys of an earlier era had been using her for target practice. Today, the dome sits atop the historic Arizona State Capitol building, home to the Arizona Capitol Museum.

Arizona's Morenci Mine is still one of the biggest sources of copper in the world.

The copper dome and the Winged Victory stand out against the desert sky.

ARIZONA STATE CAPITOL

WHAT A capitol building

WHERE 1700 W. Washington, Phoenix, Arizona

COST Free

PRO TIP Tour the Arizona Capitol Museum for more about the 48th state and you may find Arizona's first governor still at his desk.

29 THE MASCOT OF THE OFFICE COMPLEX

Why is there a cow on the office building at 51st Street and Washington?

A mere 50 years ago all the land was once one of the largest feedlots in the world. More than 300,000 head of cattle moved annually through the lot, and the cow you see on the roof of the Stockyards Restaurant is a final remnant of Phoenix's cattle ranching days. Another of Arizona's Five Cs, cattle ranching was a significant part of the state's and the city's economic foundation. The cattle-ranching king of Phoenix was once Edward A. Tovrea (the second owner of Tovrea's Castle), and his 200 acres of land was home to the Stockyards Restaurant, where he wined and dined some of the most famous cattle barons in the country. The land was purchased in 2004 by Jokake Construction. The Smith Brothers, owners of Jokake, are Arizona natives and chose to preserve the Stockyards Restaurant and keep a little piece of Phoenix history safe from the wrecking ball. Today, you can still get rocky mountain oysters and reminisce about the horse-riding, cattle-wrangling days of yore.

The original Stockyards Restaurant opened in 1947 but succumbed to a fire only a few years later. The new one was rebuilt in 1954 and stills stands to this day.

The bell to the left of the Stockyards is a replica of the Liberty Bell and was dedicated by Tovrea.

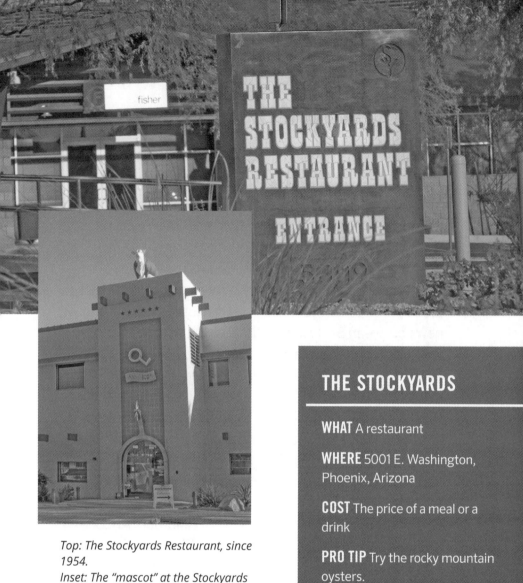

Top: *The Stockyards Restaurant, since 1954.*
Inset: *The "mascot" at the Stockyards Industrial Office Complex.*

THE STOCKYARDS

WHAT A restaurant

WHERE 5001 E. Washington, Phoenix, Arizona

COST The price of a meal or a drink

PRO TIP Try the rocky mountain oysters.

THE PONY EXPRESS RIDES AGAIN

Is mail still delivered by horse to Scottsdale?

Even by 1862 the Pony Express was an outdated concept. By then, telegraph lines had finally traversed the Midwest, connecting California and the Western territories with everyone east of the Mississippi. From 1860 until 1861, however, the Pony Express (a relay of tough horses and tougher young men spread out across 2,000 miles of dangerous terrain) ensured delivery of news between St. Joseph, Missouri, in the east and Sacramento, California, in the west. They often battled freezing weather, Indian raids, and even injury to deliver news, such as Lincoln's election and the start of the Civil War. While part of the United States, Arizona wasn't even a territory yet. The state has no real connection with the Pony Express, but in 1959, almost 100 years later, the Hashknife Sheriff's Posse in Holbrook, Arizona, decided to stage a Pony Express ride. On March 10, 27 men on 27 horses set out to deliver a letter from Holbrook, Arizona, to the state fairgrounds in Phoenix in 27 hours. The event was staged to coincide with the Jaycees' annual rodeo and parade. The following year they made the same run but into Scottsdale, carrying about a thousand pieces of U.S. mail, making the Hashknife Pony Express the oldest

When Arizona hosted the Super Bowl in 2015, Hashknife Pony Express riders delivered the Super Bowl picks to the ESPN team.

Passing the Legacy, *by Cowboy Artists of America member Herb Mignery, captures the urgency and dedication of the Pony Express riders.*

THE HASHKNIFE PONY EXPRESS

WHAT A piece of living history

WHERE Holbrook, Arizona, to Scottsdale, Arizona

COST $1 per letter (half the cost of the original Pony Express)

PRO TIP Discover more Western art at Western Spirit: Scottsdale's Museum of the West in the Marshall Arts District.

Pony Express ride sanctioned by the U.S. Postal Service to deliver mail. Every January/February, about 30 volunteer riders who are members of the Navajo County Sheriff's Posse, or sworn in as such, set out from Holbrook on horseback carrying more than 20,000 pieces of first-class mail with the "via Pony Express" postmark. During the three-day journey, they travel over the Mogollon Rim through Payson and south along the Beeline Highway (State Route 87) into Scottsdale. While its run was short, the official Pony Express bridged the communication gap between the two coasts of a quickly growing nation. Today, Arizona's annual Hashknife Pony Express ride is a piece of living history. Every year it receives letters until a few days before the ride. Check their site (www.hashknifeponyexpress.com) for the next deadline.

31 THE WEDDING CAKE HOUSE

Is that a wedding cake up there on that hill?

Not to be confused with ASU's Gammage Auditorium, which has also been called a wedding cake, this wedding cake can clearly be seen from the Loop 202 as it travels toward downtown Phoenix. Alas, it is not a wedding cake, but locals do call it the "wedding cake house," for obvious reasons. The cream-colored, multitiered "castle" (complete with an Arizona state flag sticking out of the top) was built by Italian-born, would-be hotelier Alessio Carraro, who dreamed of opening a resort in Phoenix. Carraro never did open his resort on the hill, but he did build an iconic castle that has graced the Phoenix horizon for almost 90 years. Not long after Carraro built his castle and planted his dream cactus garden, he was forced to sell the castle and property. Nearby cattle magnate E. A. Tovrea bought it for his new bride, Della, but Tovrea didn't live there for long. He died less than a year later, leaving his bride to live alone in the castle for nearly 40 years. The castle remained empty until the City of Phoenix bought it in 1993 and renovated it. Today, the castle and its beautifully landscaped grounds can be seen clearly from Washington and Van Buren Avenues and glimpsed from the Loop 202.

The Tovrea Carraro Society began giving tours in 2012.

The Arizona flag flies above Tovrea Castle.

TOVREA CASTLE AT CARRARO HEIGHTS

WHAT A tour of a unique and historic building

WHERE 5025 E. Van Buren St., Phoenix, Arizona

COST $15 per person

PRO TIP Reserve your tickets well in advance; they are very hard to come by.

WATER DOESN'T RUN THROUGH IT

Why isn't there any water in this river?

The Salt River runs directly through the Valley of the Sun, but you may not always see it full of water. In fact, most often if there's any water, it's a mere trickle between the banks, but that wasn't always the case. Before the Roosevelt Dam was finished in 1911 north and east of the city, the river often often overflowed its banks when it rained, destroying homes and farmland for miles around.

A river without any water is somewhat difficult to grasp and can be confusing for those who see the Salt River clearly outlined on any Phoenix map. Pass over several of the Valley bridges, including the one on Central Avenue just south of

SALT RIVER ALSO KNOWN AS RIO SALADO

WHAT A river

WHERE Salt River at Central Avenue

COST Free

PRO TIP Take a bike ride along the banks of the Salt River. You can pick up the path at the Nina Mason Pulliam Rio Salado Audubon Center.

The Salt River passes beneath the Loop 202 into Tempe Town Lake.

I-17, and you'll usually see a river in name only. Often, the only indicator that water is nearby is the lush green flora crowding the banks. A few other such rivers and creeks are in the area, including the Agua Fria, Gila, and New Rivers as well as Skunk Creek. These desert rivers usually have water only when it rains heavily, and then it can be quite dangerous to try to cross them. Dry washes also crisscross the Valley. These tend to overflow during heavy rains and can flood roads and bridges. Arizona has a "stupid motorist" law that states to the effect that if someone drives through a barrier to cross a flooded roadway he or she must cover the cost of their rescue.

Miles of pathways can be found along the Salt River, including Tempe's bend in the river, Tempe Town Lake.

<u>33</u> HIDDEN HAUNTS

Where are some of the Valley's spookiest places?

A city the size of Phoenix is bound to have a few ghosts and hidden haunts. One of the most well-known ghost stories is about the woman who threw herself off the rooftop at the Hotel San Carlos in downtown Phoenix.

Early in the morning of May 8, 25-year old Leone Jensen jumped to her death from the roof of the Hotel San Carlos. At the time, the local newspaper stated that it was very clearly a suicide. Jensen left behind several letters and a note, clearly saying good-bye and outlining her wishes for her impending funeral. She even indicated the reason for her suicide—a disease that was becoming too debilitating for her. Over the last seven decades, her reason for jumping has evolved into an unrequited love. Psychics who have visited the hotel claim that she had just broken up with her boyfriend, who was a bellman at the Westward Ho. They have also claimed that she was pregnant and had been murdered. According to newspaper accounts at the time, she had only been in the

Hotel San Carlos was once a favorite of Hollywood's early superstars; their stars can be found in the sidewalk outside.

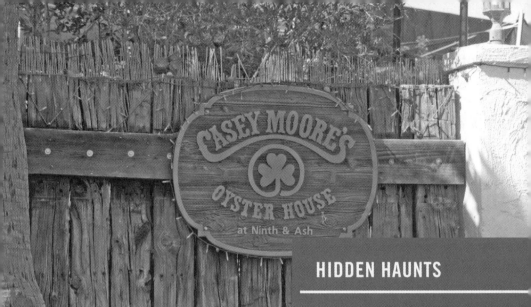

Casey Moore's in Tempe is located at the corner of 9th and Ash.

HIDDEN HAUNTS

WHAT Spooky stories

WHERE Hotel San Carlos or Casey Moore's

COST The cost of a drink or hotel stay.

PRO TIP Keep your eyes open.

Phoenix area two to three weeks, not necessarily enough time to get a boyfriend or get pregnant. Whatever the reason for her death, hers is only one of the ghosts said to haunt the historic hotel.

Another female ghost is said to haunt another historic building in another Valley City. The Tempe home where Casey Moore's Oyster Bar is now located was built before the turn of the last century and is said to be haunted by several ghosts. Employees and customers have reported seeing a hovering young woman and a dancing couple as well as flying utensils, weird orbs, and unexplained tugs and touches.

Hip Historian Marshall Shore gives local tours and talks about some of the Valley's most well-known haunts. Visit his site for more info: marshallshore.blogspot.com.

34

ARIZONA'S ODD WEATHER PATTERNS

Is that a haboob or a monsoon?

The traditional weather calamities that plague other parts of the country, such as hurricanes, tornadoes, and snowstorms, are not events that typically occur in the Arizona desert. While the Phoenix area has seen the occasional tornado and has even felt an earthquake or two—the state is home to several dormant volcanoes—our typical weather patterns tend to more closely resemble weather phenomenon found in the Middle East than they do anywhere else in the United States. The Sonoran Desert tends to whip up swirling dust devils, dangerous brownouts, torrential monsoons, and haboobs big enough to swallow a city whole.

Late summer, usually August, the Valley experiences its monsoon season, which drops most of the desert's annual rainfall. It also brings higher humidity and the heavy storms bring a symphony of lightning and rolling thunder. When these monsoon storms arrive, they come so fast and furious that the water has nowhere to go.

Monsoon comes from the Arabic word mausim, meaning "season."
Monsoon represents a seasonal shift from a dry wind to a wet wind, bringing higher precipitation. The word *haboob* is an Arabic word meaning "violent wind."

Above: Monsoons bring rain and even hail so quickly that streets flood and rivers run rapidly.
Right: A haboob looms above a Tempe neighborhood.

The ground is dry and hard-packed, and the water sits on the surface, gathering speed and power, collecting in washes and in riverbeds, flooding low-lying roads and rushing along the curbs too quickly for sewer drains to keep up.

When thunderstorm conditions suddenly dissipate due to the dry air, a vacuum is created, making way for another phenomenon— the haboob. These powerful storms pull sand and dirt up into the air, creating walls of dust almost a mile high and often more than 100 miles wide. They move at a good clip, about 30 miles an hour, and sweep the desert floor, filling the air with so much debris that a severe brownout occurs, temperatures drop, humidity rises and winds averaging 50 miles an hour whip through town. While central Arizona has been experiencing haboobs for decades, several of our more recent haboobs have earned Phoenix worldwide recognition.

MONSOONS & HABOOBS

WHAT Weather phenomenon

WHERE Across the valley

COST Free

PRO TIP Haboobs and monsoons typically occur during the hot summer months.

35

CELEBRATING CULTURAL DIVERSITY

Was there segregation in Phoenix?

Originally named the Phoenix Union Colored High School when it opened in 1926, George Washington Carver High School, as it was named in 1943, was the only high school in the city built exclusively for African American students. For almost 30 years, it served as an all-black high school, until 1953, when segregation was finally ruled unconstitutional in Arizona. In 1954, the school closed. Beginning in the mid-1990s, the school's alumni association, the Phoenix Monarchs, began the process of buying the property from the City of Phoenix, saving it from planned destruction. Their goal was to turn their old school into an African American cultural center and museum. Over the last two decades, the Phoenix Monarchs have renovated the building, bringing the space up to code.

A statue of George Washington Carver.

The Calvin C. Goode Municipal Building in downtown Phoenix is named for 1945 graduate and former city councilman Calvin Goode.

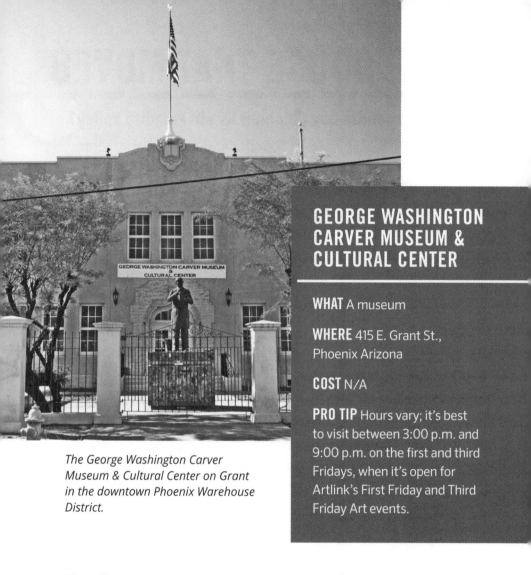

The George Washington Carver Museum & Cultural Center on Grant in the downtown Phoenix Warehouse District.

GEORGE WASHINGTON CARVER MUSEUM & CULTURAL CENTER

WHAT A museum

WHERE 415 E. Grant St., Phoenix Arizona

COST N/A

PRO TIP Hours vary; it's best to visit between 3:00 p.m. and 9:00 p.m. on the first and third Fridays, when it's open for Artlink's First Friday and Third Friday Art events.

Thus far, the museum has showcased exhibits like that from the Negro Leagues Baseball Museum and held cross-cultural events designed to raise awareness around cultural diversity. Additionally, the group, which was established in 1986, has developed plans to build permanent exhibits and meeting rooms and event space, and even landscape the school's former sports field.

Tucked away in the city's old but up-and-coming Warehouse District, the cultural center and museum are already helping to increase awareness and encourage development in the area.

36

THE HOUSE THAT MOVED

Didn't Sandra Day O'Connor live in Paradise Valley?

In 1959, Sandra Day O'Connor and her husband, John, hired local architect D. K. Taylor to design a home for them in Paradise Valley. The family lived there until 1981, raising three boys and forging the relationships and foundation for Sandra's career. In 2006, the retired Associate Supreme Court Justice discovered her old home was scheduled for demolition. As the primary residence for the first woman ever to sit on the U.S. Supreme Court, it was worth preserving, and in 2007, the City of Tempe stepped up to save it.

For two years, the home was moved, brick by adobe brick, and reassembled at a specially chosen site in Papago Park in Tempe, protecting a significant piece of U.S. and Arizona history.

Today, this little gem is hidden off Curry Road north of Tempe Town Lake at Arizona Heritage Center. The home of retired Supreme Court Justice Sandra Day O'Connor now serves as a place for civic discourse, similar to the role it served during O'Connor's rise to the Supreme Court.

Since her days as a law student at Stanford, Sandra Day O'Connor has been paving the way for women. Getting work as a female attorney proved difficult, and after a few

William H. Rehnquist, a fellow classmate at Stanford Law School, was appointed to the U.S. Supreme Court in 1972.

Left: The gravel path, Lizard Trail, passes in front of the driveway to the O'Connor House; you can find it on the south end of the parking lot at the Arizona Heritage Center at Papago Park. Right: The driveway entrance to the O'Connor House in Tempe.

SANDRA DAY O'CONNOR HOUSE

WHAT Historic home

WHERE 1230 North College Ave., Tempe, Arizona

years (some of it working for free), she and her husband settled in metro Phoenix, where she served for four years as the Assistant Attorney General of Arizona. In 1970, she was appointed to fill a state senate seat and was then elected in 1972 to fill the same seat. Once again blazing new trails, she became the first woman in any state to be elected by her peers as the Senate Majority Leader. Following her stint in the legislative branch, O'Connor served four years on the Maricopa County Superior Court and another two with the Court of Appeals. By the time Reagan appointed her to the United States Supreme Court in 1981, she had spent time as a trial attorney, a legislator, and a judge. She was approved by the U.S. Senate in September 1981 by a vote of 99-0 and served until her retirement in 2006.

37

RATTLE & YUM

Where can I taste rattlesnake?

It's a fact. A rattlesnake's bite is dangerous, painful, and potentially deadly. Anyone who has been hiking the trails in Arizona knows that the snake's telltale rattle is enough to make even the most seasoned hikers freeze in their tracks as their hearts beat double-time. What you may not know, though, is that rattlesnake is also a local delicacy in the Southwest. Often served deep-fried with a side of chipotle ranch dressing, this tasty dish can give you a new appreciation for the slithering, rattling reptile. One of the best places to try rattlesnake is at the family-owned and -operated Rustler's Rooste at the Arizona Grand Resort in Phoenix. Set on a hillside at the edge of South Mountain Park, the Western-themed restaurant serves its rattlesnake appetizer with another local delicacy, prickly pear fries.

The tarantula, Gila monster, and scorpion are a few more of the desert's creepy crawlies, but they haven't made it onto any menus . . . yet.

Rustler's Rooste near Phoenix South Mountain Park Preserve.

RATTLESNAKE

WHAT An appetizer

WHERE 8383 South 48th St., Phoenix, Arizona

COST $18.95 plus tax and tip

PRO TIP Pair the Rustler's Rooste Arizona margarita (flavored with pink, sweet prickly pear juice) with the rattlesnake appetizer.

38

PHOENIX'S GREAT DIVIDE

Did Phoenix send its Japanese citizens to internment camps?

After the attack on Pearl Harbor, Phoenix found itself on the dividing line that determined which states, cities, and regions would send their Japanese and Japanese-American citizens to internment camps that had been set up around the Western United States. While the USS *Arizona* anchor sitting upright at the east end of Wesley Bolin Plaza is a symbol of American patriotism, the memorial in Poston, Arizona (near Yuma, about 185 miles west of Phoenix), is an apology for the wave of fear that washed across the Western states during World War II. The movement, fueled by Executive Order 9066, divided the Phoenix area, sending 16,000 Japanese and Japanese-Americans to one of two internment camps beginning in early 1942. The great dividing line followed Washington Avenue in Phoenix, Apache Boulevard in Tempe, and Main Street in Mesa. Those who lived on the north side of the divide remained while those south of the line were forced into camps. One such camp was located near the Gila River not far from the current city limits of the City of Chandler.

In early 2017, the City of Chandler Museum hosted an exhibit called Un-American: Japanese Internment in our Backyard.

The Valley Metro light rail passes along Main Street in Mesa, which, along with Apache Drive in Tempe and Washington Avenue in Phoenix, once marked the dividing line.

ARIZONA'S WWII JAPANESE INTERNMENT CAMPS

WHAT A piece of WWII history

WHERE Phoenix, Tempe, and Mesa

COST Free

PRO TIP The Poston Memorial Monument in Poston, Arizona, located about 200 miles west of Phoenix, marks one of the camps.

39 THE EXOTIC BIRDS OF GLENDALE

How did peacocks get into the park?

Drive through the towering front gates of Sahuaro Ranch and you'll see the outline of a peacock above the name. It was in the 1930s that Sahuaro Ranch became known locally for its exotic birds, when Lottie Smith, lady of the house, purchased them for the property. But local legend has it that the ancestors of this particular peacock family were here at least a decade or two before Arizona became a state. Peacocks are very territorial and can still be found wandering around their ancestral home—strutting along the paths and among the citrus trees around the 80-acre historic ranch and surrounding property. The acreage was once part of a 640-acre parcel of land originally homesteaded in 1886 by William Henry Bartlett from Illinois. Over the years, it was sold off until the Smith family sold the remaining 160 acres in 1977, including 80 acres to the City of Glendale. The historic ranch shares its acreage with a public park, Glendale Community College, and the City of Glendale Library. Today, you can still catch an occasional glimpse of these birds wandering among the old structures and even across the parking lot near the library.

SAHUARO RANCH

WHAT One of the Valley's oldest farmsteads

WHERE 9802 N. 59th Ave., Glendale, Arizona

COST Free

PRO TIP Bring your smartphone/tablet with you and scan the QR codes to follow an online tour of the property.

Top Right: A peacock crosses the path from the west parking lot entrance at Sahuaro Ranch.
Above: The colorful rose garden is in full bloom in spring.

The beautiful rose garden
in front of the main and guest houses
was planted before the
turn of the 20th century.

THE RAT PACK ERA LIVES ON

Where can I swim in a martini olive-shaped pool?

To step into the Hotel Valley Ho in Scottsdale is to step into the era of Frank, Sammy, Dean, Peter, and Joey. Even after 60-plus years, the Hotel Valley Ho still evokes images of the Rat Pack with its 1950s- and '60s-era architecture, brightly colored interior, and martini olive-shaped swimming pool. Opened in 1956, the hotel was originally a two-story property and remained so until Westroc Hotels & Resorts bought the declining hotel in 2001. The architectural firm hired by the new owners retained the hotel's historic style and incorporated several fun, '50s-style touches, such as the martini olive-shaped pool. They even added the seven-story tower that now overlooks the original lobby.

Back in its original heyday, Hotel Valley Ho was a favorite location for Hollywood's finest, and more than a few weddings took place on its lush acreage, including the 1957 wedding between Robert Wagner and Natalie Wood.

The original hotel was designed by Frank Lloyd Wright student Edward L. Varney in the mid-1950s.

Top: The Hotel Valley Ho sign at the corner of 69th Street and Main Street.
Above: The 1950s-era Hotel Valley Ho in Scottsdale.

HOTEL VALLEY HO

WHAT A historic, midcentury hotel

WHERE 6850 E. Main St., Scottsdale, Arizona

COST $19.56

PRO TIP For an architectural tour of the property, consider Scottsdale's Ultimate Art & Cultural Tours' Magical History Tour.

41 TOUCH THE STARS

Where can I journey into the universe?

Arizona State University is home to several one-of-a-kind museums and exhibits. One of its most stunning and probably best-hidden experiences can be found in the unassuming Interdisciplinary Science and Technology Building 4 on the university's Tempe campus. At 300,000 square feet, the building is the largest of ASU's research facilities and home to six different schools, including the School of Earth and Space Exploration. Not just any school, the SESE, as it is known at ASU, melds together the teachings and research of eight diverse disciplines, including cosmology, geosciences and planetary sciences, exploration systems engineering, science education, astronomy, and astrophysics. The results have been astounding. More importantly, the SESE is dedicated to sharing what they've discovered with the public, and they do that in a small 250-seat auditorium known as the Marston Exploration Theater. The Marston is not your average school auditorium. It's not even a cutting-edge movie theater. Instead, it's a 3D gateway into the universe and beyond. The theater offers four different 60-minute, three-dimensional, narrated tours that take attendees beyond our solar system, beyond our galaxy, and into the far-reaching corners of our universe. Twice a week and for special occasions, the theater opens to the public. Don a pair of 3D glasses, and find the stars, planets, and galaxies close enough to touch.

In addition to the four 3D shows, members of the SESE faculty offer lectures.

MARSTON EXPLORATION THEATER

WHAT A journey into the stars

WHERE 781 S. Terrace Rd., Tempe, Arizona

COST $7.50 per adult

PRO TIP The four shows alternate between Wednesdays at 7:30 p.m. and Saturdays at 2:30 p.m.

Top: The Marston Exploration Theater box office at Interdisciplinary Science and Technology Building 4 in Tempe. Inset: Air Apparent by James Turrell on ASU's Tempe Campus.

Air Apparent, another of ASU's hidden secrets, is a short walk from the theater. Head east toward Rural Road along the walkway from the Interdisciplinary Science and Technology Building's main entrance.

THE WORLD'S 4TH TALLEST FOUNTAIN

Was Fountain Hills really named after a giant fountain?

The town of Fountain Hills gives the term "master-planned community" new meaning. In the late 1960s, the founder of Fountain Hills, Roger McCulloch, an architect and developer from McCulloch Properties, a subsidiary of McCulloch Oils, decided that something spectacular might draw folks to the outer edges of the McDowell Mountains. The fountain was designed to be a centerpiece for the community, "making it visible for miles." The towering fountain was completed in 1970, and the town of Fountain Hills grew up around it. Today, 23,000 residents call it home.

The fountain, which is said to be the fourth tallest fountain in the world, only reaches its tallest height of 560 feet three times a year, including St. Patrick's Day (when the fountain turns green), the 4th of July, and December 5 in celebration of the city's date of incorporation. Every other day it hits heights of more than 300 feet every hour on the hour from 9:00 a.m. until 9:00 p.m. The fountain and lake are located in a beautiful 64-acre park in the center of Fountain Hills.

Roger McCulloch is the same architect who brought the London Bridge to Lake Havasu City, Arizona, in 1968.

FOUNTAIN PARK

WHAT A fountain and lake

WHERE 12925 N. Saguaro Blvd., Fountain Hills, Arizona

COST Free

PRO TIP Arrive a few minutes before the hour; sometimes it starts a little early. The fountain will not run on windy days.

Top: Walking paths traverse Fountain Park.
Above: The fountain at Fountain Hills.

43 A LYRIC-INSPIRING STRETCH OF ARIZONA HIGHWAY

Is Carefree Highway the same highway that inspired Gordon Lightfoot's song?

The 30-mile stretch of State Route 74, known locally as Carefree Highway, wends its way through a disappearing section of the Sonoran Desert west of Phoenix. The highway was immortalized by the Canadian folk singer Gordon Lightfoot in 1973. Tooling along in his rental car while traveling through Arizona, Lightfoot was inspired by the sign he saw and apparently scribbled the lyrics to his Billboard-topping hit before he even left the state. Carefree Highway was originally built in 1964 to connect Interstate 17 with U.S. Highway 60 to Wickenburg. It was meant to be a temporary highway, but in 1989 that was laid to rest. Today, Carefree Highway extends east to Tom Darlington Drive, which is also known as Scottsdale Road farther south.

"Carefree Highway" hit #10 on the Billboard charts in 1973.

CAREFREE HIGHWAY

WHAT An inspiring highway

WHERE Highway 74, or Carefree Highway

COST Free

PRO TIP You can pick up Carefree Highway off I-17 and take it west to Lake Pleasant.

*Top: Carefree Highway winding through the Sonoran Desert west of Phoenix.
Above: The sign for the Carefree Highway exit to Lake Pleasant.*

GOLDFIELD GHOST TOWN (page 20)

SONORAN DOG AT THE LODGE (page 46)

A HABOOB (page 70)

HASHKNIFE PONY EXPRESS (page 62)

USS *ARIZONA* AND USS *MISSOURI* GUNS (page 128)

WORLD'S 4TH TALLEST FOUNTAIN (page 86)

DIVING LADY MOTEL (page 184)

SAGUARO CACTUS (page 194)

PHOENIX ARROW (page 186)

PHOENIX SENTRIES AT OLD CITY HALL (page 206)

SALT RIVER (page 66)

GEORGE WASHINGTON CARVER MUSEUM (page 72)

MEMORIAL HALL (page 162)

PAPAGO PARK ROCKS (page 112)

EISENDRETH HOUSE (page 30)

AN OLD MOUNTAIN'S NEW NAME

Who is Lori Piestewa?

Originally named Squaw Peak, Piestewa Peak was renamed in 2003 for Lori Piestewa. The renaming of the iconic peak in north central Phoenix put to rest a decades-long controversy around the term "squaw" and honored a woman who sacrificed her life for her country. Pfc. Lori Ann Piestewa was the first Native American woman to die in combat on foreign soil. The 24-year-old Hopi woman from Tuba City, Arizona, died on March 23, 2003, in an

ambush in Iraq. This same ambush left eight other soldiers dead and led to the imprisonment of several members of the 507th Maintenance Company, including Spc. Shoshana Johnson and Pfc. Jessica Lynch.

The panoramic city view from Piestewa Peak.

Arizona State Route 51 was also renamed from Squaw Peak Parkway to Piestewa Freeway.

Looking north from the top of Piestewa Peak.

PIESTEWA PEAK

WHAT A mountain

WHERE Phoenix, Arizona

COST Free

PRO TIP Stay on the trail and off the rocks.

Piestewa Peak, part of the Phoenix Mountain Preserve, is located north of Lincoln Avenue and east of State Route 51, now known as Piestewa Freeway. The stairstep-style climb of the summit trail is a little over one mile up and ascends 1,200 feet to the top of the peak. The path is considered moderately difficult, but you may get lapped by local runners who use the path for training purposes. Early mornings during the week tend to offer the least amount of traffic. Spots along the trail offer places to catch your breath and the view. The peak and preserve offer several additional hikes of varying degrees of difficulty and distance.

The switchback path of Summit Trail.

45 EARN YOUR WINGS

Where can I test my mettle as a fighter pilot?

Phoenix-Mesa Gateway Airport in Mesa was known as Williams Air Force Base during World War II. Like Falcon Field to the north, it was converted from an air base to an airfield but not until the base closed in 1993. In its 52-year history, almost 27,000 men and women learned to fly. Today, as a public airfield, it offers a different type of training experience.

If you've ever dreamed of being Iceman or Maverick in the 1986 movie *Top Gun*, this is your chance. While you won't be climbing the skies in the U.S. Air Force's multimillion dollar fighter jets, you will get firsthand "combat" experience. The Mesa-based Fighter Pilot International offers you the closest you'll get to chasing enemy planes across the blue skies. Climb straight into the sky with their flight and combat flight packages. Learn how to chase your opponent, outmaneuver your enemy, and test your grit (and your stomach) in a series of in-air combat situations. Their specially designed aerobatic aircraft can roll, dive, and climb quickly, giving you top spot in the hot seat.

FIGHTER PILOT INTERNATIONAL

WHAT Fighter flight experience

WHERE 5865 S. Sossaman Rd., Mesa, Arizona

COST $915 intro per person

PRO TIP The 2-Day Combination Adventure Package offers both flight and combat experience.

Above: Phoenix-Mesa Gateway Airport.
Left: The T-38A Talon from the entrance at Williams Air Force Base.

One fighter jet is left at Phoenix-Mesa Gateway Airport. The T-38A Talon on display when Williams Air Force Base was still a base is now on permanent display at Lt. Charles L. Williams Memorial Park on the airport grounds.

The base was originally named for Lt. Charles L. Williams, a pilot who died in 1927.

GIANT RED ROCKS

What are those giant red rocks in the middle of Phoenix?

The massive red sandstone buttes sitting along Galvin Parkway straddling both Phoenix and Tempe baffle most folks who first see them. Geologists say they were formed millions of years ago. In more recent years, the area has been designated an Indian reservation, a temporary national monument, and even a prisoner of war camp during World War II. Today, the municipal park is home to the Phoenix Zoo, Desert Botanical Garden, and Hunt's Tomb. It is also home to Hole-in-the-Rock, another unique natural rock formation. As far back as Phoenix is old, the Hole-in-the-Rock has served as a landmark along the Phoenix/Tempe border.

Today, it is the prize at the end of a very short

but steep hike. From the formation, you can see much of the 1,100-acre park, which has several man-made attributes as well. Families picnic at the ramadas, and children climb giant stone desert animals, such as the tortoise and the Gila monster. An archery range is also

Galvin Parkway is named after Paul Galvin, founder of Motorola.

PAPAGO PARK RED ROCKS

WHAT A unique rock formation

WHERE 625 N. Galvin Pkwy., Phoenix, Arizona

COST Free

PRO TIP The 2.3-mile Double Butte Loop travels around two of the park's red rock buttes.

Top: The Papago Butte along Galvin Parkway.
Above: Hole-in-the-Rock at Papago Park.

available, as well as an eight-acre lagoon, four easy hiking trails, and the Hall of Flame—another of the Valley's best kept secrets.

47 MEMBERSHIP HAS ITS PRIVILEGES

Why is there a $5 membership fee on my bill at the Wrigley Mansion?

The Wrigley Mansion Club, as it has been called for the last few decades, sits high above the Arizona Biltmore Resort in Phoenix. Once the sprawling winter "cottage" of the famous Wrigley family, it now hosts a restaurant, bar, and daily tours. The stunning architecture, 1920s furniture, hardwood floors, and floor-to-ceiling windows remain—capturing a bygone era. Situated in one of the city's most luxurious residential areas, the mansion is required by city statute to maintain its private club status. In 1992, when George "Geordie" Hormel (of the Hormel meatpacking family) and his wife, Jamie, bought the mansion, they wanted to open it to the public. Local homeowners revolted, and the city refused to change the old zoning restrictions. The Hormels found a way around it. That $5 addition to your bill is a trial membership fee to the "exclusive" Wrigley Mansion Club. Membership does have its privileges: the $15 annual fee means complimentary valet parking and a drive up the steep hillside rather than a walk.

Today, guests can eat brunch, lunch, or dinner in what was once the grand living room of the Wrigley family's winter home, grab a glass of wine at Jamie's Wine Bar, or wend their way through the majestic halls on a guided tour.

The view from the Wrigley Mansion is a panorama of the city.

The view from the south side of Wrigley Mansion.

WRIGLEY MANSION

WHAT A private club

WHERE 2501 East Telawa Trail

COST Memberships start at $15/year

PRO TIP Pair one of the club's tours with a meal for the full Wrigley Mansion experience.

Above: The Wrigley Mansion Club, perched above the Arizona Biltmore Resort and golf course.
Left: A sign points the way to the entrance of the Wrigley Mansion Club.

48 THE MYSTERY ROOM AT THE ARIZONA BILTMORE

Can I still grab a drink in the Mystery Room at the Biltmore?

The biggest mystery about this room may be when it's open for business. Over the last couple of years, the Mystery Room has gained quite a bit of local recognition for its Prohibition-era happy hours. Built at the height of Prohibition, the Arizona Biltmore, located in one of the Valley's wealthiest neighborhoods, was perfect for sneaking a drink. History has it that the Mystery Room was designed specifically to hide the resort's speakeasy—complete with a secret bar that turns into a bookcase. For a time, speakeasy nights, as they were called, happened on Sunday evenings, and clues to the secret password were shared through Twitter as the event drew nearer. Most recently, the resort's speakeasy events have been held the last Friday of the month. Either way the room is a perfect location for a manhattan or an old fashioned.

Follow the resort's Twitter account @ArizonaBiltmore for tips on the next speakeasy event.

MYSTERY ROOM AT THE ARIZONA BILTMORE

WHAT A secret speakeasy

WHERE 2400 E. Missouri Ave., Phoenix, Arizona

COST The price of a drink

PRO TIP The room is hidden in the main building.

The Arizona Biltmore opened in 1929.

49

PHOENIX'S FIRST CITY CENTER

Who or what is Luhrs?

The Luhrs family was one of the Salt River Valley's earliest developers. George H. N. Luhrs purchased the property south of Jefferson in the mid-1880s. He built the Luhrs Hotel, which is no longer, and he and his son, George Luhrs Jr., built two of the city's earliest "skyscrapers"—the Luhrs Building in 1924 and the Lurhs Tower in 1929. Both buildings rose during one of the city's biggest growth spurts. The Luhrs Tower represents the Art Deco architectural style mirrored in many of the buildings erected in the latter 1920s. Others include the City-County Building and Orpheum Theatre. The tower was originally meant to be 12 stories

when the original plans were completed in 1928, but when it opened in 1929 there were 14 stories, and it quickly became one of the most iconic buildings of the Phoenix skyline. In Alfred Hitchcock's 1960 film *Psycho*, the opening scene pans the downtown Phoenix skyline. Several of the city's oldest buildings were featured. As the camera zooms in on the Barrister Building where the hotel scene takes place, the Luhrs Building can be seen on the right-hand side of the screen.

Bitter & Twisted, a local craft cocktail bar, sits at the northwest corner of the Luhrs Building

Today, the Luhrs Building and Luhrs Tower are part of the Luhrs City Center complex. A developer purchased both properties in 2007 with plans to add a hotel. The buildings now house restaurants, retail space, and offices, such as the craft cocktail bar Bitter & Twisted.

The entrance of Luhrs Tower off Jefferson Avenue.

The seven-story Heard Building was also featured in the opening scene of *Psycho*. It's the building with the radio tower on its roof.

119

50

FROM OWLS TO SUN DEVILS

What's a Sun Devil?

Arizona State University in Tempe has been through a few names in its 100-year-plus history. When it first opened in 1885, Arizona was only a territory and more than 25 years away from becoming a state. The school was first known as the Territorial Normal School at Tempe. In 1901, it became the Normal School of Arizona. Then it became Tempe State Teachers College, the Arizona State Teachers College, and in 1945 Arizona State College. It wasn't until 1958 that the school received university status and finally became Arizona State University. It's no surprise that as the school name evolved, so did its mascot. Student athletes at the school had been known as the Normals, the Bulldogs, and for a time the Owls before they became the Sun Devils.

The term "sun devil" is often synonymous with the weather phenomenon known as a dust devil. The more Southwest-sounding name seemed to appeal to the students, who voted in the fall of 1946 to leave behind the Bulldogs and embrace the Sun Devils. No one seems to be able to exactly pinpoint who first suggested the name, but in November 1946, Arizona

---

It is said that Sparky's facial characteristics are based loosely on Walt Disney, Anthony's boss at the time.

Arizona State University, home of the Sun Devils.

State College played its last game as the Bulldogs and became forever known as the Sun Devils.

Sparky, the Sun Devils' mascot, was designed by ASU alumnus and Disney illustrator Berk Anthony in 1948.

SPARKY THE SUN DEVIL

WHAT ASU's college mascot

WHERE Across ASU campuses

PRO TIP You'll catch Sparky at any ASU sporting event.

51

THE END OF A LINE

Why can't you travel to Phoenix by train?

The sixth-largest city in the country, Phoenix, is one of only a few major cities in the United States that you cannot access by commuter train, but that wasn't always the case. At one time, you could take the Sunset Limited from the East Coast through Phoenix and on to Los Angeles on the West Coast. In the latter part of the 1980s, Amtrak added Tempe as a stop along the Sunset Limited route, hoping to capitalize on ASU's growing student population. The City of Tempe refurbished the old Southern Pacific depot on Ash Avenue only to close it less than 10 years later. In 1996, when Amtrak's contract with Southern Pacific expired, Phoenix decided not to spend the money necessary to keep the commuter train service running. As a result, Amtrak pulled out of Phoenix and Tempe and then, a couple of years later, rerouted the Sunset Limited through the City of Maricopa about 30 miles south of Phoenix.

Phoenix Union Station, located at 4th Avenue and Harrison Street, was originally built in 1923 and funded

Phoenix Union Station fenced in at 4th Avenue and Harrison Street.

Above: The Valley Metro Light Rail train now passes alongside the front of the Depot Cantina.
Inset: The restaurant has a caboose patio for private parties.

PHOENIX UNION STATION

WHAT A piece of railway history

WHERE 401 West Harrison St., Phoenix, Arizona

COST Free

PRO TIP Pick up the Sunset Limited in Maricopa, Arizona, or the Southwest Chief in Flagstaff.

by several railroads running through the area, including the Santa Fe Railroad and an affiliate of Southern Pacific. Today, it is considered permanently closed. Tempe's old depot, however, has been put to good use. In the late 1990s, Macayo's, a local and well-known Mexican restaurant, opened Depot Cantina, preserving a piece of Tempe's train history.

Macayo's lays claim to another Arizona gem: the chimichanga, which Macayo's says they invented when an employee accidentally dropped a burrito into the deep fryer.
A happy accident, indeed!

52

THE MURDER OF DON BOLLES

Does Phoenix have ties to the mob?

In the early 1960s, the name Don Bolles began appearing as a byline under the titles of some of *The Arizona Republic*'s most controversial political articles. An investigative reporter, Bolles sought to uncover organized crime and political scandal in Phoenix at the time. Close to Vegas, the desert city was thought by some to serve as a vital access point for some of Sin City's mob-driven activity. Bolles had noted the comings and goings of some of the mob's biggest crime family members and had notecards filled with details on anyone he thought was related, including local businessmen, developers, and ranchers. It is thought that Kemper Marley, one such rancher, put a hit out on Bolles because he smeared him in the news. To this day, while there is plenty of speculation, no one knows if it was a local power broker, such as Marley, or a bigger player, such as a mobster from Vegas, NYC, or Chicago, pulling the strings.

In Phoenix, the Clarendon Hotel is considered the site of one of the most gruesome, mob-related crimes. On June 3, 1976, when Don Bolles realized that his

Don Bolles died on June 13, 1976, days after the bomb exploded. His murder is included on the murder wall at the Mob Museum in Las Vegas.

The front entrance of the Clarendon Hotel.

source, who was a low-level criminal named John Adamson, was a no-show, he left the lobby and got back into his white Datsun. Before he could back out of the space in the parking lot, a remote-controlled bomb planted below the front seat of his car exploded. In his agony, Bolles uttered a few last words that witnesses can't quite seem to agree on. It is no question that Adamson lured Bolles to the Clarendon late that morning or that he placed the remote-controlled bomb beneath Bolles's car as it sat in the parking lot of the hotel. Adamson was convicted of second-degree murder in exchange for naming Jimmy Robison (muscle for hire and the man who pushed the button) and Max Dunlap (a local businessman involved in scandal). Both were later convicted of killing Bolles and conspiring to murder Attorney General Bruce Babbitt (who would later go on to become governor) and a businessman named Al Lizanetz.

53

THE SOFTEST OF ARIZONA'S FIVE Cs

Are those cotton fields along the highway?

Cotton is another one of Arizona's famous "Five Cs." During the height of Arizona's cotton boom, the state was covered with 800,000 acres of long-staple cotton. Today, that number is closer to 200,000 acres, but about 900 cotton farmers are still in the region. During World War I, Goodyear Tire and Rubber Company recognized that Arizona land was perfect for growing cotton and bought 16,000 acres. Soft, durable, long-staple cotton was perfect for making airplane tires. Today, most Arizona cotton farmers grow short-staple cotton, but cotton is still an integral piece of Arizona's economic makeup. In fact, Supima, a long-staple variety that is extra-long and considered one of the world's finest cottons, is grown in Arizona. Pima cotton was cultivated with the help of the Pima Indians, and Supima, developed in 1954, is an amalgamation of the words "superior" and "Pima". Supima cotton can be found in major brands, such as Brooks Brothers and Bloomingdale's.

The Goodyear Tire and Rubber Company used Pima cotton for tires on bicycles, cars, and airplanes.

Goodyear, Arizona, was founded by the Goodyear Tire and Rubber Company.

COTTON FARMS

WHAT Farmland

WHERE Maricopa and Pima Counties

COST Free

PRO TIP You'll see cotton bolls appear in fields late summer/ early fall.

54 THE USS *ARIZONA* COMES HOME

Why is there a giant anchor in the middle of downtown Phoenix?

An anchor in the middle of the desert is an eye-catching display. This one holds special meaning, not just for Arizonans but also for Americans. When the USS *Arizona* set out to sea in the mid-1910s, she was strong, solid, and capable. The attack on Pearl Harbor diminished her to a crumpled, sunken heap. To this day, she remains at the bottom of the Pacific Ocean, a national shrine to the men who died aboard the ship. Of the 1,216 on board that day, only 39 survived. In December 1976, one of the battleship's anchors was brought to Arizona—a monument to that day and to those men. The 10-ton anchor sits at the east end of Wesley Bolin Plaza, encircled by 12 plaques recounting each of the men who lost his life. Another monument on the Plaza features guns from both the USS *Arizona* (the start of the war) and the USS *Missouri*, which had a significant role in the last days of World War II.

Wesley Bolin Plaza, an open park space in the heart of Phoenix's government district, features more than 30 such memorials and monuments, including war memorials to the Korean War, Vietnam, and World War II, as well as a memorial to those who died on 9/11.

The USS Arizona was dedicated in 1914 by then Governor W. P. Hunt.

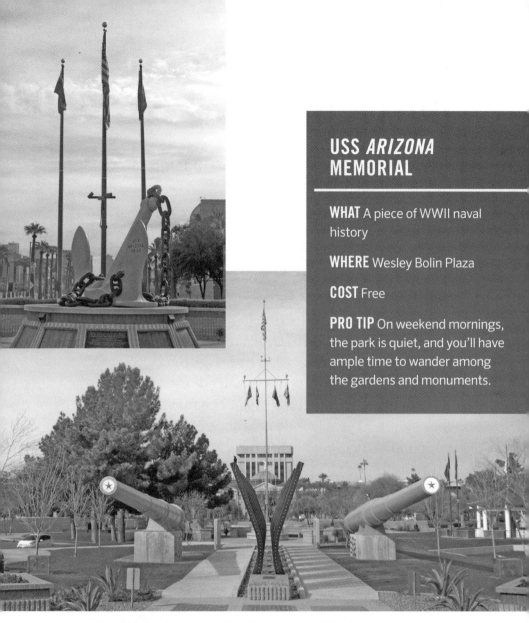

USS *ARIZONA* MEMORIAL

WHAT A piece of WWII naval history

WHERE Wesley Bolin Plaza

COST Free

PRO TIP On weekend mornings, the park is quiet, and you'll have ample time to wander among the gardens and monuments.

Top: The USS Arizona's *anchor sits at the east end of Wesley Bolin Plaza.*
Above: The battleship guns from the USS Missouri *and USS* Arizona. *The state capitol building rises in the distance.*

55 A PRETTY LITTLE DOLLHOUSE

Why is there a life-size dollhouse in Tempe's industrial corridor?

Located at the northwest corner of Priest Drive and Southern Avenue in Petersen Park is the old Petersen House. The home of Danish immigrant, banker, entrepreneur, and rancher Neils Petersen and his family, it is the oldest example of Queen Anne-style residential brick architecture in the Valley. The home was designed during Arizona's territorial days by well-known Arizona architect James Creighton in 1892. At the time, American architects had adopted England's Victorian-era architectural style. The movement lasted only about 30 years, and just a couple of examples can be found in the Phoenix area.

Creighton was a productive architect throughout his 40-year career in Arizona. He went on to design commercial and public properties. Many of his buildings, such as the original Phoenix City Hall and Tempe City Hall, have since been demolished, but others, for example, the Pinal County Courthouse in Florence and the Carnegie Public Library just west of downtown Phoenix, are still standing. In Tempe,

---

The Rosson House is another example of the Queen Anne Victorian-style home. It's located at Heritage Square in downtown Phoenix.

THE PETERSEN HOUSE

WHAT Queen Anne-style residential brick architecture

WHERE 1414 W. Southern Ave., Tempe, Arizona

COST $5 per person (for groups of 10 or more)

PRO TIP To schedule group tours, contact 480-350-5100 or museum@tempe.gov.

Top: The Petersen House at Southern & Priest in Tempe.
Above: The president's house at ASU's Tempe campus.

Creighton also designed the president's house at ASU, where the Virginia G. Piper Center for Creative Writing is now located, and the Andre Building and Odd Fellows Hall in downtown Tempe, both of which now serve as retail and office space on Mill Avenue. He also designed the Suhwaro Hotel on Buffalo Street in Chandler, across from another historic building, the San Marcos Resort. Built in 1916, the Suhwaro Hotel was renovated in 1999 and is now home to retail space and restaurants in downtown Chandler.

56

THE VALLEY'S WATERWAYS

Why are so many canals here?

Phoenix was aptly named. In the latter half of the 19th century, it literally rose again from the ashes of an earlier civilization—one that had farmed the area for almost a thousand years. To this day, no one knows exactly why these ancient Sonoran Desert people,or Hohokam as later tribes called them, disappeared around the year 1450. (There is speculation that years of drought finally drove them away.) Whatever the reason, they left behind hundreds of miles of empty waterways. In the 1860s, Arizona settlers passing through the area quickly recognized the meaning of these old ditches—the promise of fertile land—and they began excavating the existing canals and digging new ones. The Grand Canal, the area's oldest canal, was built by the Grand Canal Company about the same time Phoenix was founded in 1868. These canals diverted tons of water to farms across the region, revitalizing the Valley. Today, many of the canals are managed by the utility company SRP and continue to deliver water across the metropolitan area.

Water is an attractive quality in the desert, and the canal system creates ribbons of oases throughout the Valley. You won't find any gondolas on these canals, but

The Valley was originally settled by the Hohokam, a Pima Indian word that means "those who came before."

THE CANALS

WHAT A water delivery system

WHERE Across the Valley

COST Free

PRO TIP Rack up the miles; use SRP's distance calculator at srpnet.com/water/canals/distances.aspx.

Above: The Crosscut Canal runs alongside Papago Park.
Right: This path runs along the Crosscut Canal, which was built in 1888, and connects the Arizona and Grand Canals.

many wide pathways run alongside, making them a favorite place for Valley residents and tourists to walk, run, and bike. If you look closely, you'll find canals intersecting major thoroughfares, such as Baseline Road in the East Valley, 67th Avenue and 19th Avenue in the West Valley, and all points in between. One of the longest canals, the Arizona Canal, runs almost 70 miles across the Valley from Surprise in the west to the Salt River Pima-Maricopa Indian Community in the east.

57

DURANT'S "HIDDEN" FRONT DOOR

Where is the front door at Durant's?

Everyone who is anyone (this means locals, longtime residents, and even seasonal tourists, of which there are many) knows to use the back door at Durant's. In fact, if you ask most people where the front door is located, chances are they would have to think about it. Occasionally, you'll see of a handful of confused individuals standing in the shadows just beyond the hostess stand, blinking the bright, desert sunlight out of their eyes. Right behind them would be the front door. From the outside, it's a nondescript wooden door with a brass handle in the shape of a "J" and an intersecting "D." The pink-and-black tile scheme of the recessed entryway blends with the pink stucco walls. Scuffed black-and-maroon tiles lead from the concrete sidewalk up to the door jamb. There's even a maroon awning over the sidewalk in front that says Durant's in white script. From Central Avenue, if you're speeding by in a car or lumbering along on the light rail, you may catch a glimpse and think, "Oh, that's where it is!" But as for going in, you'll most likely forget about it and pull into the lot off of Virginia and stroll through the real entrance—the one to the kitchen.

Durant's, originally owned by the very cool and colorful Jack Durant (Hollywood even made a movie about him), opened in 1950 when Phoenix was still a small town and martinis could be ordered with lunch. Durant may or may not have had ties to the mob. No one seems to know, but he was a gregarious although

Durant's on Central Avenue in Phoenix.

DURANT'S

WHAT A local landmark

WHERE 2611 N. Central Ave., Phoenix, Arizona

COST Cost of a meal

PRO TIP You can reach the back door from the back parking lot off Virginia Avenue.

Durant's front door off Central Avenue.

private man, and he kept his friends close and his cards closer. Durant died in 1987, but the family-owned restaurant has maintained Durant's promise of great steaks, the best booze, and good friends. They've even kept the same style of interior decor.

Hollywood made a movie about the restaurant's "mysterious" owner Jack Durant in 2016—*Durant's Never Closes.*

58

NATIVE AMERICAN LANDS

Are there Indian reservations in Phoenix?

Arizona is nearly 114,000 square miles, and 27 percent, or 20 million acres, comprises tribal lands controlled by 21 different tribes. Several of these reservations are located in and around the Phoenix area, representing the Maricopa, Pima, and Yavapai Indians. The tribes have built and manage a series of casinos and resorts in and around the Valley and are host to some of the best resorts and restaurants in the state. The AAA Four Diamond Sheraton Grand at Wild Horse Pass, owned by the Gila River Indian Community, is home to Kai, the state's only AAA Five Diamond restaurant. On the other side of town near Scottsdale is the high-rise hotel Talking Stick Resort as well as the Cactus League's newest spring training park—Salt River Fields at Talking Stick. Near Fountain Hills, nestled among the McDowell Mountains, is the 24,000-acre Fort McDowell Yavapai Nation. The small tribe continues to farm its ancestral land and owns and manages the Fort McDowell Casino.

Loop 101, as it passes from Tempe into Scottsdale, travels through the Salt River Pima-Maricopa Indian Community. The Pima and Maricopa Indian tribes have developed the property on either side of the highway, building gas stations, casinos, resorts, and several shopping and entertainment complexes.

Orange Sky, the restaurant on the top floor of the Talking Stick Resort, features a stunning view of the Salt River Pima-Maricopa Indian Community's tribal land.

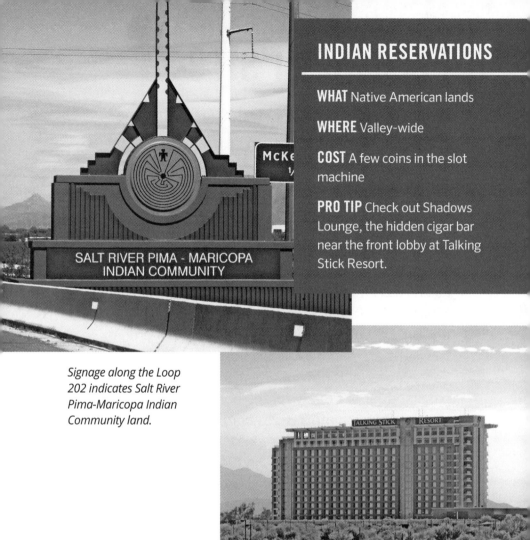

INDIAN RESERVATIONS

WHAT Native American lands

WHERE Valley-wide

COST A few coins in the slot machine

PRO TIP Check out Shadows Lounge, the hidden cigar bar near the front lobby at Talking Stick Resort.

Signage along the Loop 202 indicates Salt River Pima-Maricopa Indian Community land.

Talking Stick Resort, located on Salt River Pima-Maricopa Indian Community land.

59 FLY LIKE IT'S 1942

Where can I fly in an old World War II airplane?

With more sunny days than just about any other city in the country, Phoenix is an ideal place for flying. During World War II, the U.S. military recognized this and placed bases and airfields across the Salt River Valley. For several years, American and Royal Air Force pilots practiced their craft above the mountainous desert floor. Today, most of those bases have been converted into public airfields and even a school (Thunderbird), but at Falcon Field, you can still fly like it's 1942. The hands-on flight experience offered by the flight crew at the Arizona Commemorative Air Force Museum is not your typical museum visit. These old planes aren't ready for the boneyard yet, and that means climbing into a B-25J bomber or C-47 cargo plane and heading into the skies.

When the airfield opened in 1941, the Mesa Chamber of Commerce ran a contest to choose a name. Of the 100 that were submitted, they chose one of the suggestions—Falcon Field. The word "falcon" aptly represented the well-known bird of prey as well as the American and RAF pilots hunting down enemy planes.

Today, seven active military bases are located in Arizona, including Luke Air Force Base west of Phoenix.

Arizona Commemorative Air Force Museum at the northeast corner of Greenfield Road and McKellips Road.

ARIZONA COMMEMORATIVE AIR FORCE MUSEUM

WHAT An interactive WWII flight experience

WHERE 2017 N. Greenfield Rd., Mesa, Arizona

COST Museum tickets $15 per adult; flights $150 per person

PRO TIP Reserve your special flights in advance.

<u>60</u> IT'S A DRY HEAT!

How hot does it really get in Phoenix?

Some old booster saying from the 1930s says: "Welcome to Arizona, where summer spends the winter, and hell spends the summer." And it's possible that hell would feel right at home in the intense summer heat that Phoenicians endure from about May until September, depending on the year. Weather.com says Phoenix, on average, sees 110 days per year of 100 degrees or more. That kind of heat often inspires the question: "How hot is too hot?" You may hear a number anywhere from 108 to 113 degrees. While many Phoenicians love the dry heat (average annual humidity is less than 40%; in June it drops much lower), it can get too hot even without the humidity. In recent years, the city has seen temperatures as high as 119 degrees, but it wasn't all that long ago that the Valley saw temps up over 120 degrees. On that day, June 26, 1990, it was so hot that even the local politicians had to joke about it. Legend has it that Arizona historian Marshall Trimble ran a contest among the local mayors. Instead of "your mamma" jokes, the mayors competed to create the best "It's so hot . . ." jokes. Mayors from

---

The hottest day on record was June 26, 1990, when the mercury hit 122 degrees.

140

The hottest day on record in Phoenix was recorded at Phoenix Sky Harbor International Airport.

Paradise Valley and Scottsdale were runners-up to Tempe Mayor Harry Mitchell, who claimed, "It was so hot that he saw a saguaro pull itself up by its roots, walk over, and hunker down in the shade of a mesquite tree." Sometimes it is so hot that you'll see pigeons standing in the shade.

THE HOTTEST DAY ON RECORD

WHAT Legendary heat

WHERE Phoenix, Arizona

COST Our heat is free

PRO TIP The desert is so dry that drinking plenty of water year-round is a must.

61 PHOENIX WAREHOUSE DISTRICT RISES

What are those WD signs for in downtown Phoenix?

The warehouse district, which straddles the railroad tracks through central Phoenix, was once the epicenter of transportation for the entire Valley's thriving produce industry. The WD signs above the street signs at intersections throughout the area indicate locals' efforts at revitalization. For decades, the district had been an empty and dilapidated part of town, and for a while

its biggest contribution was cheap parking for sports fans. The two-mile stretch from 7th Avenue to 7th Street along the railroad tracks looks at the backside of both Chase Field (originally Bank One Ballpark, or BOB) and Talking Stick Arena (formerly known as America West Arena and US Airways Center). On game days, owners of empty lots put up sandwich boards with hand-painted signs—$5 or $10 parking.

In 2017, Denver-based Galvanize converted the old General Sales Co. warehouse into a 120,000-square-foot mixed-use campus for adult STEM training programs, coworking, and office space.

Top: Galvanize's new campus at 515 E. Grant in the Warehouse District.
Above: The Duce is the converted Anchor Manufacturing Company building, constructed in 1925.

THE WAREHOUSE DISTRICT

WHAT A growing business and entertainment district

WHERE 7th Street to 7th Avenue between Jackson and Lincoln Streets

COST Free

PRO TIP Step inside the Duce for a look at how the Anchor Manufacturing building has been converted into a hip, new downtown spot.

Today, 15 historic buildings have been brought back into use, and several are now inhabited by some of Phoenix's brightest start-up and tech businesses, such as WebPT and Coplex; retail space; art galleries, such as Bentley Gallery; and such restaurants and bars as The Duce.

Short for produce, "the Duce" was a nickname for the city's old produce district, but some say the nickname was "the Deuce," as in the city's beat, where cops often found themselves rounding up troublemakers. The owners of the new Duce say that the old building was once a speakeasy by night and a warehouse by day. Today, The Duce is a mixed-use converted warehouse, with a boxing ring, bar, restaurant, and retail space, at the northeast corner of Central Avenue and Lincoln Street.

SCOTTSDALE'S HIDDEN ART COMPOUND

Where can I watch Scottsdale artists at work?

Tucked away in a little patch of the Sonoran Desert north of McDonald Drive in Scottsdale is an 80-year-old artists' compound. During the day, a stroll through the sprawling tract of land will bring you in touch with painters, photographers, and even a blacksmith capturing the artistic spirit of the Old West. For years, the little artist community was hidden along Cattletrack Road, impossible to find amid the Sonoran Desert landscape and hidden within a quiet residential neighborhood. Quite a departure from the sleek, modern galleries of the Marshall Arts District, Cattle Track hasn't changed all that much from its inception in the late 1930s when George and Rachael Ellis bought the property and later created an artists' retreat. Today, the compound, while just as secluded, is a little easier to find. Creatives, such as Western photographer Scott Baxter, ceramics artist and former tennis pro Mary Van Dusen, and welder and metal sculptor Ron Hagerty

---

Philip Curtis, founder of the Phoenix Art Museum, worked at the compound from the 1940s until he died in 2000.

The sign for Cattle Track Arts Compound is hidden on Cattletrack Road.

CATTLE TRACK ARTS COMPOUND

WHAT An artists' community

WHERE 6105 N. Cattletrack Rd., Scottsdale, Arizona.

COST Free

PRO TIP The best time for a visit is during events.

work out of the various galleries and studios. The compound hosts exhibitions, events, and music concerts and has compiled projects highlighting the work of its historic artists, including the fashion work of Rachael Ellis.

63 TEMPE'S BURIED HISTORY

Where are all of Tempe's famous people buried?

Tempe's first cemetery is hidden on the west side of the ragged buttes situated alongside Interstate 10 where it merges with U.S. 60. The area was once considered the outer edges of Tempe; today, it's in a forgotten strip of town west of I-10 that most assume is part of South Phoenix. Named for Double Butte Mountain, which serves as a backdrop to the cemetery, Double Butte Cemetery includes burials as old as 1888 when the land was donated by Neils Petersen, but the cemetery didn't officially open until 1897. It is the final resting place for several of Tempe's early mayors. You will also find famous Tempeans, such as father-son duo Charles Trumbull Hayden, who is credited with founding Tempe, and his son, Senator Carl Trumbull Hayden, who served Arizona for almost 60 years in Washington, D.C., first as a representative and later as a senator. In the pioneer section, you'll find the town's first doctors, Gregg and Moeur. Moeur also served as Tempe's mayor and one of Arizona's early governors. Another Arizona governor buried in this cemetery is John Howard Pyle, who served a four-year term as the state's ninth governor. Pyle's claim to fame is that he was the first Arizona governor born in the 20th century.

Double Butte Cemetery is open sunrise to sunset.

146

Sunrise at Double Butte Cemetery.

DOUBLE BUTTE CEMETERY

WHAT Tempe's pioneer cemetery

WHERE 2505 W. Broadway Rd., Tempe, Arizona

COST Free

PRO TIP The pioneer section of the cemetery is immediately to the left when you enter off Broadway.

The Memorial Garden at Double Butte Cemetery.

THE DESERT IN SPRING

When does the desert bloom?

One of the desert's best-kept secrets is that in spring it blooms into a beautiful, bountiful garden of color. This typically happens in March/April, and the number of plants in bloom relies heavily on the amount of rain that falls in the cooler winter months. Yellow seems to be the predominant color, and you will see it splashed against the mountains and hillsides as brittlebrush, marigolds, poppies, daisies, and sunflowers run riot across the landscape. Look closely and you'll also see the pink flowers of the beavertail prickly pear cactus, the red and yellow blooms of the desert prickly pear, and the orange-red clusters atop the spiny shoots of the ocotillo. Pink and orange globe mallow, purple lupine, and bluebells add their own dashes of color. In gardens, in the cracks in the sidewalks, among the pebbles beside paved paths, spring arrives in a spray of color—yellow, red, purple, pink, orange. Trees sport an assortment of hues, for example, the bright yellow blooms of the palo verde tree, the pale blue berries of the juniper, and the small white blossoms of the orange tree. Landscaped streets and strip malls sprout mounds of yellow, orange, and red lantana, while bright pink bougainvilleas climb walls, and the deep yellow and orange trumpet flowers of the orange jubilee hang heavily over brick fences. Take a drive out

Catch wildflower fever in spring
(usually March or April).

Top: The desert in bloom along Beeline Highway south of Fountain Hills.
Inset: Beavertail prickly pear in bloom along the Salt River in south Phoenix.

along Beeline Highway (also known as AZ 87) north of Mesa up to Fountain Hills or drive east out U.S. Highway 60 past Apache Junction toward Globe and Superior for a glimpse of the desert in bloom. Some of the best places to see Mother Nature's colorful display are right in the middle of the Phoenix metro area, including Desert Botanical Garden at Papago Park and the Nina Mason Pulliam Rio Salado Audubon Center in south Phoenix.

65 THE FIRST MCDONALD'S THAT ONCE WAS

Is the Yoshi's building the site of the first McDonald's in Phoenix?

Central Avenue was once a type of burger paradise. In the mid-20th century, "cruising Central" was one of the favorite pastimes of the era's American teens, and for a time, big burger joints, such as McDonald's, Bob's Big Boys, and others, crowded the city's main thoroughfare. Today, most of those burger places are gone. Even the city's first McDonald's restaurant didn't survive the march of progress. When the fast-food restaurant opened at the southwest corner of Indian School Road and Central Avenue in 1953, it was the very first McDonald's franchise in the world. While Ray Kroc was still a few years away from systematizing the McDonald brothers' burger business, the brothers themselves were already working to franchise their concept. Their first franchisee, Neil Fox, a Phoenix doctor, and his two business partners opened the city's first McDonald's across the street from what is now the light rail's Central and Indian School station. They bought the license for a mere $1,000, sold their burgers

At the time, it was said that a McD's could churn out six hundred hamburgers an hour.

Yoshi's at the corner of Central Avenue and Indian School Road, where the city's first McDonald's once stood.

for 15¢ apiece, and were the first to use those iconic golden arches.

Today, the site where McDonald's once stood is now Yoshi's, a fast-food Asian restaurant.

YOSHI'S

WHAT The site of the first McDonald's franchise.

WHERE 4050 Central Ave., Phoenix, Arizona

COST Free

66

THE OLD HOUSE IN TEMPE

How did the house where Senator Hayden was born become a steakhouse?

Once considered the oldest continuously occupied structure in the Valley, Monti's La Casa Vieja finally closed in 2014. The local steakhouse began as the home of Charles T. Hayden, founder of Hayden's Ferry, which later became the City of Tempe. The adobe-brick, Sonoran-style row house was built in 1873. In 1877, it also became the birthplace of Arizona's native son Carl T. Hayden, who served his home state as a U.S. Congressman for 15 years and a U.S. Senator for 42 years.

In 1889, when Carl was only 12, the Hayden family moved out and began calling it "the old house," or *la casa vieja*. The Hayden House was expanded and operated as a boarding house until 1920, when two of Hayden's sisters decided to have it restored to its original 13-room, L-shaped structure that stretched along Mill Avenue and 1st Avenue. In 1924, they opened it as a teahouse and restaurant, and Leonard Monti purchased it in 1954. In 1956, he opened it as Monti's La Casa Vieja, a steakhouse. For almost 60 years, Carl's old home housed one of the best steakhouses in the Valley.

The Ostrich in Chandler rescued Monti's wraparound booths when the restaurant closed in 2014.

Top: One Hundred Mill signage indicates developer plans to build around the historic site.
Inset: The Monti's sign off Mill Avenue before the restaurant closed in 2014.

MONTI'S LA CASA VIEJA

WHAT A piece of Tempe and Arizona history

WHERE 100 S. Mill Ave., Tempe, Arizona

COST Free

PRO TIP Monti's backroom (you'll see an entrance off the back parking lot) was known as the place to meet with Tempe's movers and shakers.

Along with its delicious steaks, the iconic restaurant served a mouthwatering, house-made Roman bread. Served with every meal, the bread, sprinkled with rosemary and salt, became one of the restaurant's staples and a favorite among regulars. Despite its popularity, rising costs forced Leonard's son, Michael, to sell the restaurant. The current owners expect to build a 200-plus-room hotel and retain the old house as part of the new space, promising to preserve the historic old home and the history it represents.

67

THE VALLEY'S HIDDEN HALL

Where can I see a fire "engine" from 1725?

The Hall of Flame may be one of the Valley's best-kept secrets. Tucked away in a corner of Papago Park on the dividing line between Tempe and Phoenix, the 30,000-square-foot museum is ablaze with some of firefighting's coolest tools and oldest engines. Where else would you find the ornately decorated, horse-drawn parade carriages from the late 19th century? To walk through the museum's collections is to take a tour through the history of firefighting from the early part of the 18th-century through today. The horse-drawn carts, motorized engines, hand-pumpers, tools, and paraphernalia showcase firefighter efforts the world over. The massive collection highlights pieces from Germany, France, Japan, and England as well as historic engines and wagons from cities across the United States.

Arizona has had its share of wildly out-of-control wildfires, and the museum showcases the efforts these specially trained firefighters make to curb the miles-wide fires that threaten lives, land, and homes.

The museum also has a tribute to the uniformed men and women who lost their lives on 9/11.

The Hall of Flame museum at Papago Park.

HALL OF FLAME

WHAT A museum for the history of firefighting

WHERE 6101 East Van Buren St., Phoenix, Arizona

COST $7

PRO TIP Get your picture taken on the 1952 fire engine.

68

URBAN BIRDWATCHING

Where can I see a snowbird?

Sun City west of Phoenix is a sure place to see the seasonal tourist known locally as the snowbird. The term used for retirees who migrate from colder weather to warmer climes and back again is a regular occurrence in Arizona. In 1960, Del Webb gave retirees a reason to stay. "With 50 years or more, they're your entry fee for membership into an exclusive and active new-way-of-life . . ." was the announcement seen in local papers in the days leading up to the community's grand opening. The king of the master-planned community, Del Webb made national news on January 1, 1960, when he opened Del Webb's Sun City to a lengthy line of eager retirees looking for paradise. Within the first week, more than 100,000 visitors had flocked to the oasis in the desert for a look at the five model homes the Del Webb company had constructed. The idea of an active retirement community certainly appealed to the 50-and-older crowd and still does to this day.

SUN CITY, ARIZONA

WHAT An active adult community

WHERE Sun City, Arizona

COST Free

Welcome to Sun City.

The landscaped streets of Sun City.

In the last 60 years, Sun City has expanded to include almost 40,000 residents, eight golf courses, and seven recreation centers, offering countless clubs, classes, and events.

While Sun City was the first of its kind, countless other active adult communities (they're no longer called retirement communities) are located in and around the Phoenix metropolitan area.

Before Del Webb got his hands on the land, Sun City was fields of cotton and alfalfa.

69 THE LAND WITHOUT DAYLIGHT SAVING TIME

Wait. What time is it?

When our smartphones today are often smarter than we are, it's a surprise when your phone fails to recognize that the imaginary line that separates Pacific Standard Time from Mountain Standard Time does not apply to Arizona. Daylight Saving Time dates back to 1918, as an effort to support the nation during the First World War.

By 1919, it was repealed as a national measure. Then, for the duration of U.S. involvement in World War II, Americans set their clocks an hour ahead. It wasn't until 1966 that DST was revisited. Arizona went along to get along for about two years before the state legislature voted to ignore it. As a result, Arizona's time never changes. In March, when the rest of the country springs forward, Arizona stays exactly where it is, putting it in the same time zone as the Pacific coast. When the United States falls back in November, the Mountain states join Arizona, and the state finds itself an hour ahead of the Pacific coast.

Not everyone in Arizona declines to spring forward or fall back. The Navajo Nation observes Daylight Saving Time.

A spring sunrise in Tempe. In summer, Arizonans have an extra hour before the summer sun blazes.

WHAT An Arizona tradition

WHERE State-wide except the Navajo Nation

COST Free

PRO TIP In spring, Arizona is three hours behind the East Coast, and in fall it's only two hours behind.

159

70 EAU DE ORANGE BLOSSOM

What is that deliciously heady smell every spring?

In 1909, the *Arizona Republic* published a public discourse on the pros and cons of planting additional orange groves. At the time, citrus was one of Arizona's original Five Cs and a pillar of the state's economic foundation. The Valley was already acres and acres of citrus groves—orange, grapefruit, and lemon. At the height of Arizona's citrus boom, more than 80,000 acres were farmed. As the metropolitan area grew, however, the land beneath the orange trees eventually became a more lucrative proposition than the oranges themselves, and our miles of orange groves have slowly been replaced by tracts of master-planned communities. Today, citrus groves can still be found in metro Phoenix. New developments, for example, those along McKellips Road in Mesa, retained some of the trees along the borders of their neighborhoods, and homeowners have taken to planting citrus trees as part of their landscaping. Every spring you can still smell the heavenly scent of orange blossoms in the air.

While the scent of orange blossoms still abounds, the boxes of "free" oranges, lemons, and grapefruits once commonplace along street curbs are rarely seen. However, more than one coworker still brings in a Basha's

Peaches are another local favorite; the short season lasts only a few weeks in late spring.

CITRUS GROVES

WHAT One of Arizona's Five Cs

WHERE Valley-wide

COST Free

PRO TIP Take a walk after dark in early spring to catch a whiff, or drive down McKellips in Mesa for a glimpse of citrus trees.

Top: Lemon trees grow in an old orchard at Sahuaro Ranch Park in Glendale.
Right: Sake Bomber in Tempe makes a freshly squeezed Orange Slice Martini every spring with locally grown oranges.

grocery bag full of fresh fruit from their backyard trees every year, and neighborhood restaurants continue to use these fresh local ingredients to dress up their seasonal menus. While the Phoenix metropolitan area is no longer a top contributor to citrus production in the state, Arizona remains a significant U.S. source of lemons, tangerines, oranges, and grapefruits.

71

BOARDING SCHOOL FOR INDIAN STUDENTS

What was the Indian School?

It's no surprise that Steele Indian School Park is located on Indian School Road just off Central Avenue in what is called Encanto Village. What may be surprising is that the school itself was aptly named. Beginning in the latter part of the 19th century, the U.S. government sent Native American children from 23 tribes across the Southwest to what was then called the United States Industrial Indian School. The goal was to assimilate them into the "American" way of life. Over the decades, the student band and choral groups became well known for their local performances, and many local Native Americans have memories of the school and their time there. The boarding school finally closed in 1988, and the City of Phoenix acquired the 160-acre property in 1996. After a lot of haggling, voting, and public outcry, the city relinquished 85 acres to commercial development

STEELE INDIAN SCHOOL PARK

WHAT A 75-acre park in Midtown

WHERE Entrance is at 7th Street & Indian School Road

COST Free

PRO TIP Columns along the Circle of Life walkway provide a historical account of the school.

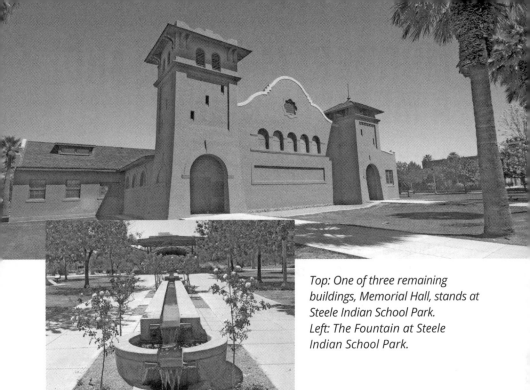

Top: One of three remaining buildings, Memorial Hall, stands at Steele Indian School Park.
Left: The Fountain at Steele Indian School Park.

and an expansion of the Veterans Hospital among other things, leaving about 75 acres to set aside for a city park. In 2001, the city opened the first 50 acres, complete with winding paths, a beautiful waterfall, and dedications from the Native American culture. Of the original school and its buildings, only three remain. Two of the buildings will be renovated as a museum and Native American cultural center in the coming years.

The park is named after Horace C. Steele, whose foundation donated $2.5 million to the renovation of the park.

72

MURDER, MAYHEM, AND A MEDICAL CLINIC

What is the Grunow Clinic on McDowell Avenue?

The Lois Grunow Memorial Clinic, as it was originally called, has a couple of claims to fame. First, the intricate design of its facade and the Spanish Colonial Revival architecture are distinctive enough to garner attention from observant motorists on McDowell Avenue. Second, the clinic was one of the first of its kind in Arizona when it opened in 1931. The clinic was built in honor of Lois Anita Grunow, a young girl who died after a possible misdiagnosis. The clinic was endowed with a $1 million grant by her father to offer doctors access to lab resources and patients easier access to care. Stunning murals here depict key scientific discoveries, and the clinic also features a marble floor and beautifully painted ceiling. It's third, and perhaps biggest, claim to fame, is that Winnie Ruth Judd, one of Phoenix's most notorious criminals, was one of the clinic's earliest employees. Known for decades as the Trunk Murderess, Judd tried to escape to California by train to cover up the murders of her two friends, whom she may or may not have killed in cold blood. The jury never decided if she was guilty of murder, manslaughter, or even self-defense, but she was locked up in the state mental hospital for almost 40 years. She escaped six times, including once for

---

In 1992, Arizona journalist Jana Bommersbach wrote about Winnie Ruth Judd and her story in The Trunk Murderess.

The Lois Grunow Memorial Clinic building at 9th Street and McDowell.

several years, before she was finally released on parole in 1971. Almost 90 years after the Judd media circus, the building continues to be a place for doctor's offices and laboratories just down the street from the ever-expanding Banner-University Medical Center Phoenix.

73 PHOENIX'S PLATFORM MOUND

Why is this pile of dirt so important?

It may seem strange to put a wall around a huge pile of dirt in the center of a big city and even stranger to build a museum around it, but this massive mound of red desert earth at the Phoenix Pueblo Museum is just about all that's left of the urban center the Hohokam began building over 1,100 years ago. If you look closely, you can see the telltale sign of the bricks that once formed the mound. This flat-top dirt pile is known as a platform mound, and the Salt River Valley's earliest settlers used it as a centerpiece for their villages.

If you climb up to the observation area, you'll see a much different view from the one the area's earliest inhabitants first saw. Situated between AZ 143 and Sky Harbor International Airport, the mound offers a look at a rapidly growing metropolitan city. Take the museum's outdoor trail for a look at the sunken ball court, adobe pithouses, excavated walls, and a view from the platform mound.

This man-made platform mound, about the size of a football field, is one of only three left in the area.

The outline of bricks stand out against the platform mound.

PUEBLO GRANDE MUSEUM ARCHEOLOGICAL PARK

WHAT A museum

WHERE 4619 E. Washington St., Phoenix, Arizona

COST $3-$6 / person

PRO TIP Start in the museum's theater for an overview of what you'll encounter.

THE BARRIO THAT IS NO LONGER

Why is there a church in the middle of that parking lot?

Golden Gate Barrio, a Mexican-American neighborhood cleared by the City of Phoenix in the mid-1970s and early 1980s, once stood between 16th and 24th Streets between Buckeye Road and I-17. As Phoenix Sky Harbor Airport expanded and added new plane routes, the city decided that the old neighborhood had to go. Over a period of about 10 years as the airport expanded, more and more families were relocated away from the barrio. Reluctant to leave, they continued to come back to the church, which was the center of their community. By 1981, it seemed inevitable that Sacred Heart would be destroyed along with the rest of the dwindling neighborhood. Residents rallied to protect the church from impending doom. With a series of meetings, signed petitions, and an intense sense of community spirit, residents convinced the City of Phoenix that Sacred Heart should be allowed to remain standing.

Today, the empty parking lot and fenced church are all that remain. The church, which was known as

---

By the end of the mass exodus, the City of Phoenix purchased 800 acres of land and relocated 6,000 people and 200 businesses.

Top: Sacred Heart Church with Chase Field in the background.
Right: The empty parking lot that was once the Golden Gate Barrio.

Sacred Heart Church, served as the community's Catholic church for decades. Funded by families in the barrio and surrounding areas, the church was built in 1954 to connect the Hispanic community.

How did the barrio get its name? One old story claims that the barrio was dubbed "Golden Gate" because one of the Valley's early Mexican families built a house on the tract of land. Others assumed that the family must have been rich to build a home and began calling the area Golden Gate.

GOLDEN GATE BARRIO

WHAT A historic Hispanic neighborhood

WHERE 919 S. 16th St., Phoenix, Arizona

COST Free

PRO TIP Sacred Heart Church opens for Christmas Mass once a year.

75 THE LONGEST-RUNNING CHILDREN'S SHOW

Who are those clowns?

Unless you are among the small percentage of Arizonans born and raised in the 48th state, you probably have no clue who these clowns are. The mural, repainted by muralist Hugo Medina on the south wall of First Studio near the Roosevelt Row Arts District, is a tribute to the 35-year legacy of local kids' television classic *The Wallace & Ladmo Show*. Dubbed the "masterpiece of morning mayhem" by *The Arizona Republic* in 1984, the show entertained both children and adults for nearly four decades. The mural depicts Bill Thompson, who played Wallace, or Wall-boy, and Ladimir Kwiatkowski, known on the show as Ladmo. Behind them is Pat McMahon as bratty little rich kid Gerald Springer, whom the audience loved to hate. Gerald was only one of several hilarious characters McMahon played in his 30 years as part of the show. The comedic trio's funny commentary, entertaining skits, and various costumed characters (including the kid-hating clown, Boffo) poked fun at everything from Eisenhower to rock and roll to cowboys. The mural was originally created in wheatpaste by local artists Nomas, Casebeer, and Jenny Ignaszewski (also known as Iggy) in 2012.

First Studio was the original home of KPHO, Arizona's first television station.

The Wallace and Ladmo mural on the south wall of First Studio located at 1st Avenue and McKinley Street.

THE WALLACE & LADMO SHOW

WHAT A mural

WHERE 631 N. 1st Ave., Phoenix, Arizona

COST Free

PRO TIP Approach First Studio from 1st Avenue for a full view of the mural.

76 THE TOWER-TOPPED HOTEL ON CENTRAL

What's the building with the giant radio tower on it?

The very distinct profile of the Westward Ho is hard to miss. Regaled as the city's tallest building until 1960, it towered over Central Avenue for more than three decades. Add the 268-foot broadcast tower (leftover from the building's days as home to KPHO-TV), and it's a memorable part of the downtown Phoenix skyline. At the time, it was one of the Valley's first premier hotels. Over its time as a hotel, it saw such presidents as JFK; Hollywood stars such as Marilyn Monroe; and even the famous and infamous, for example, Amelia Earhart and Al Capone. The owners aptly named the hotel Westward Ho hoping to inspire visitors to come West, and on opening day, the *Arizona Republic* deemed it a "magnificent monument to Arizona's progress." When the doors opened on December 15, 1928, the $2.5 million hotel was the first in the country to provide refrigerated air in its guest rooms (a long-awaited amenity for any Phoenix visitor).

In the last 90 years, the hotel's Renaissance Revival architectural style and detailed stone scrollwork can still be seen from the outside. The interior design elements,

In the late 1970s and early 1980s, the historic hotel was purchased by its current owners, who began providing affordable housing to seniors and the disabled.

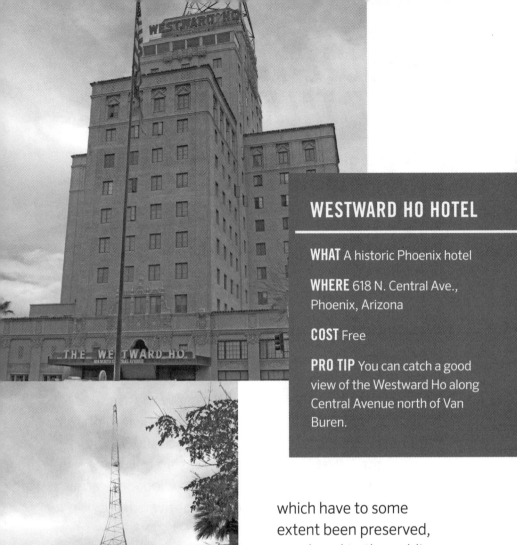

which have to some extent been preserved, are closed to the public since the building now offers private housing. In 2015, the building underwent a multimillion dollar renovation project. Fortunately, the current owners continue to preserve and restore this magnificent monument to Phoenix history.

Top: The beautifully carved Westward Ho entrance off Fillmore Avenue.
Above: The Westward Ho and the old KPHO-TV broadcast tower.

77 *TRIBUTE TO NAVAJO CODE TALKERS*

What is the giant statue at the corner of Thomas and Central Avenues?

The giant statue shows a young Native American boy sitting up. One knee is cocked, and on it he rests his elbow. In his hand, he holds a flute. The 10-foot-tall bronze statue at the northeast corner of Thomas and Central Avenues was crafted by well-known Native American artist Doug Hyde. The statue was the first of its kind—the country's very first tribute to the Navajo "code talkers." Unveiled in 1989 just a few years after President Ronald Reagan had revealed the hard work and sacrifice of 400 Navajo men during World War II, the statue is a tribute to the code talkers' role in winning the war on the Pacific front. Their code, based on key words in the Navajo language to represent military terms, proved to be impenetrable by the Japanese army and gave the United States the competitive edge it needed to win the war.

A second monument to the Navajo code talkers is located at Wesley Bolin Plaza in front of the Arizona State Capitol and depicts a Native American man in full military gear, a pack with an antenna on his back, and a radio in his hand. Designed by a Prescott-based firm, the monument carries the names of all 400-plus men and was unveiled in 2008.

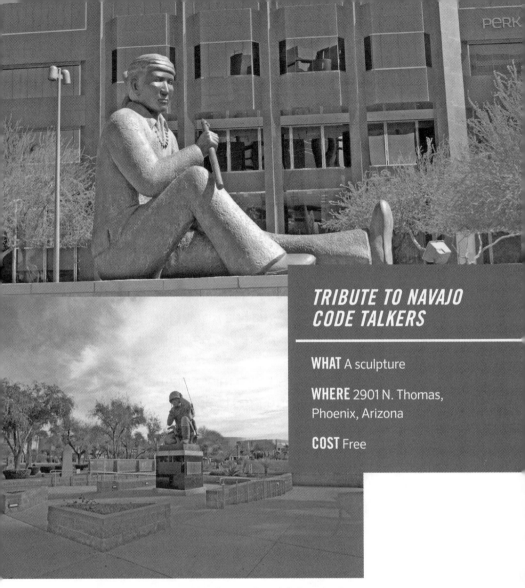

TRIBUTE TO NAVAJO CODE TALKERS

WHAT A sculpture

WHERE 2901 N. Thomas, Phoenix, Arizona

COST Free

Top: Tribute to Navajo Code Talkers in front of Phoenix Plaza in downtown Phoenix.
Above: The Navajo Code Talker Monument at Wesley Bolin Plaza.

Hyde studied under Allan Houser, another well-known Native American artist.

78

A WILD ENCOUNTER

Where might I find wild donkeys in Phoenix?

Like all lakes in the Phoenix area, Lake Pleasant is man-made. Part of the Maricopa County Parks System, Lake Pleasant formed when the Old Waddell Dam was built in 1927. At first, it was a small, 3,000-acre lake; however, in 1994 the New Waddell Dam was finished, expanding the lake to 10,000 acres and making it ideal for boating, fishing, water skiing, and even scuba diving. Tucked into the Sonoran Desert about 40 miles west of Phoenix and the Agua Fria River, Lake Pleasant Regional Park is a popular place for camping, hiking, and off-roading.

While there was never much mining in the area despite numerous attempts to do so, several archaeological digs have been made. Among the sites dating back to between 700 and 1400 AD are two small villages and a farmhouse.

Located out along the dipping, winding Carefree Highway, you can visit the marina or head farther west to Hot Springs Castle Road. Turn right and not long after the turnoff you'll see a yellow road sign with a picture of a donkey on it. Along with the animal's outline, it says "five miles." Heed its warning. These animals are descendants of the first burros brought over with the Spaniards in the 17th century. Today, herds of them roam the mountains (and roads) around Lake Pleasant Regional Park. Locals seem to have mixed feelings about these wild burros; some have argued to reduce their population and others to protect the roaming herds.

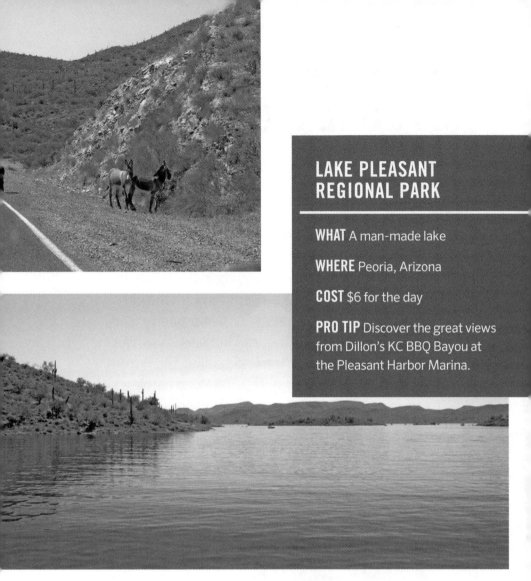

LAKE PLEASANT REGIONAL PARK

WHAT A man-made lake

WHERE Peoria, Arizona

COST $6 for the day

PRO TIP Discover the great views from Dillon's KC BBQ Bayou at the Pleasant Harbor Marina.

Top: Donkeys block Castle Hot Springs Road near Lake Pleasant.
Above: A view of Lake Pleasant from Castle Creek Drive.

Drive slowly along Hot Springs Castle Road. It's not unheard of to be stopped by a wild burro crossing.

79

BLOSSOMS OF A BYGONE ERA

Where have all the flowers gone?

The flood of master-planned communities across the Salt River Valley hit the South Phoenix area hard. Only minutes from the city's center and settled against the South Mountain Park Preserve, the area was an ideal location for new homebuilding in the 1990s and early 2000s. As developers swept through the old neighborhoods, landowners sold their property. This included the Japanese-American families known for growing acres of fresh flowers and selling them from their roadside stands along Baseline Road between 24th Street and 48th Street. For decades, every spring, tourists and residents would flock to Baseline Road, capturing the sights and smells of the colorful acreage stretching north to South Mountain. These families were known locally as the Japanese flower growers.

Beginning in the 1920s, several Japanese immigrant families settled in the South Mountain area and began

BASELINE FLOWERS

WHAT Florist

WHERE 3801 East Baseline Road, Phoenix, Arizona

COST Free to browse

South Phoenix was also known for its citrus groves and orange trees that once crowded along Baseline Road.

Top: Baseline Flowers, on Baseline in South Phoenix, is the last flower shop of its kind.
Right: The bus stop at 24th Street and Baseline reminds residents of the flower fields that once flourished north of Baseline Road.

growing vegetables. At the height of World War II, many of those families were uprooted and sent to internment camps and were unable to return to their land once the war was over. When they finally resettled, further east of town, they began adding flowers to their vegetable fields. Year after year the acreage and their reputation for colorful, fresh flowers grew. Two of the oldest families of flower growers were the Nakagawas and Kishiyamas; they were also among the last to leave. The Nakagawas' original flower stand, which they fully enclosed in 1969, remains today on Baseline Road—one of the last remnants of a beautiful family tradition.

80 NATIVE AMERICAN NOSH

It's not a tortilla, so what is it?

It's not a tortilla, pita, naan, or even Ethiopian injera. It's similar in that it's flat, round, and made to carry sweet or savory foods. Indian fry bread, similar in so many ways to the world's cultural "breads," is different, too. Like the tortilla, it's usually fried in butter or lard in a skillet, but where the tortilla is thin, fry bread is thicker, more like a pita. Yet, it's lighter, too, like naan, but not quite as crispy. Instead, it's soft, airy, light, and like all the others, quite delicious. But Indian fry bread has a heavy past. It originated when the Native American tribes were forced to use U.S. military rations (flour, lard, and sugar) to survive the 300-mile trek from their homes in Arizona to a new reservation in New Mexico. The Navajos were the first to develop the tasty bread, and it was quickly picked up by other tribes in the Southwest, including the Pima Indians, or Tohono O'odham, south of Phoenix.

Today, it's a staple of the Native American diet and integrated into everyday meals as well as important festivals. It can be folded around ground meat and taco-style fixings or drizzled with honey and sprinkled with cinnamon and sugar for dessert—it's quite good either way. The local Fry Bread House in Central Phoenix has

---

The Fry Bread House achieved national recognition in 2012 when it won the James Beard Foundation's "America's Classics" category.

The Fry Bread House in the Melrose District of Phoenix.

FRY BREAD HOUSE

WHAT A Navajo tradition

WHERE 4545 N. 7th Ave., Phoenix, Arizona

COST $6-$10

PRO TIP Bring a friend so that you can try a little of each—one savory and one sweet.

elevated the Native American fare to center stage, gaining worldwide attention with a nod from the James Beard Foundation. Opened in 1992 by Cecilia Miller (a member of the Tohono O'odham tribe) and her husband, Joedd, the little shop has grown from a handful of tables to 25. You can also find fry bread around town served fresh from the Emerson Fry Bread food truck and on more than one local chef's Southwest-inspired menu.

81

FARM HEAVEN

What is Agritopia®?

An agricultural utopia, Agritopia is a mixed-use community in south Gilbert championed by Arizona native, businessman, and restaurateur Joe Johnston. The 160-acre master-planned community offers more than a mere nod to the area's agricultural history. Established on land that once comprised Johnston's family farm and boyhood home, Agritopia is a mix of residential lots, farmland, and several restaurants. It is also home to Joe's Farm Grill, which serves a mix of comfort foods from the '50s and '60s, with a few unique twists, such as the peanut butter, strawberry, and banana sandwich and the seasonal date shake. The property also features a coffee shop and an urban farm as well as a chicken coop and an orange grove.

The real hidden gem may very well be Barnone, the community's maker space secreted at the back of the property. Wander past the farm grill and coffee shop and beyond the Johnston family farm buildings (now converted into space for the weekly farmers market) toward the giant Quonset hut-style building. Barnone houses several small craftsmen, including a florist, paper company, bakery, brewery, and wine bar.

Several of Joe's Farm Grill specialties were featured on the Food Network's *Diners, Drive-Ins and Dives* with Guy Fieri. Can you guess which ones?

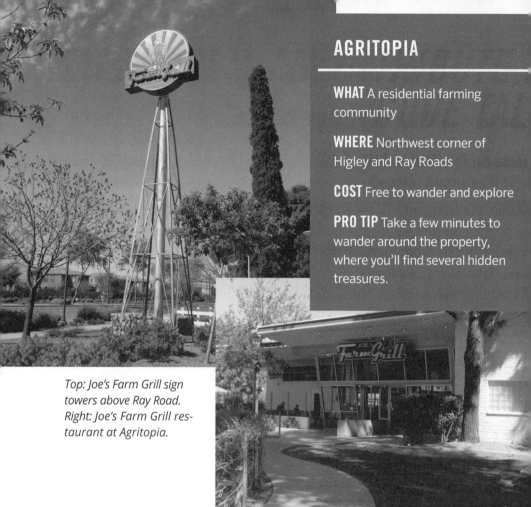

AGRITOPIA

WHAT A residential farming community

WHERE Northwest corner of Higley and Ray Roads

COST Free to wander and explore

PRO TIP Take a few minutes to wander around the property, where you'll find several hidden treasures.

Top: Joe's Farm Grill sign towers above Ray Road. Right: Joe's Farm Grill restaurant at Agritopia.

Barnone maker space at Agritopia.

82

MESA'S NEON NIGHTLIFE

Who is the Diving Lady?

According to local historians, the Diving Lady at the Starlite Motel is one of the most iconic neon signs in

the Phoenix area. She can be seen "diving" into the Starlite Motel along Main Street west of Lindsay Road in Mesa. The area is cluttered with roadside motels, their neon signs beckoning drivers off the dusty road for the night. At least, that's how it once was. Long before we used our smartphones to determine our next stops, the carefully designed architectural marvels that are the neon signs of the 1940s, '50s, and '60s captured the weary traveler's eye.

U.S. 60 once stretched end to end almost 400 miles across Arizona, an integral link between North Carolina on the East Coast and LA on the West Coast. While not nearly as celebrated as the Mother Road, it still had its share of motorists traveling the country, and the neon lights of Mesa's Main Street (the original thoroughfare for historic routes U.S. 60-70-80) beckoned. Today, many of those same motels still light up Mesa's night

Roadside sign along Main Street in Mesa marks historic routes for U.S. 60-70-80.

Paul Millet first worked for the Guerrero Lindsey Sign Company, also in Mesa, and taught Larry Graham of Graham Neon, who fixed the Diving Lady when she fell in 2010.

THE DIVING LADY

WHAT A historic neon sign

WHERE 2710 E. Main St., Mesa, Arizona

COST Free

PRO TIP Take a night drive down Main Street in Mesa. A few of these old neon signs still light the sky.

*Left: The Diving Lady at the Starlite Motel.
Right: Motel signs stand out along
Main Street.*

sky. The most well known of them is probably the Diving Lady—a seven-story work of art created by Mesa signmaker Paul Millet and his company, the Paul Millet Sign Co.

In 2010, the Diving Lady was almost lost forever. She fell victim to a thunderstorm, shattering against the parking lot below. Together, the Mesa Preservation Foundation and Graham Neon, a neon sign-making and repair shop in Mesa, put all the pieces back together again, restoring her to her former glory in 2013.

83

PHOENIX IS THATAWAY

Which way to Phoenix?

One might think that "X" marks the spot, but on Usery Mountain in east Mesa, a giant white arrow formed by the word "Phoenix" points the way. The story of the Phoenix Arrow, as the sign is locally known, is a legend of sorts (if legend implies that no one is quite sure anymore how it got there). The giant arrow is said to be a thousand feet long and a hundred feet tall. The bright white letters stand out against the dark mountain rocks. You can see it clearly if you're traveling north on Loop 202. Some say it was placed during World War II to guide the Valley's numerous fighter pilots back to the city, and some say it was a community service project for a group of Boy Scouts. A third story is a blend of both and claims that an old World War II veteran pilot wanted other flyers to have a clear path to Sky Harbor Airport. He rallied a troop of Boy Scouts to paint and carry the rocks into formation over a two-year period. More recent stories claim that it took the Boy Scouts five years, not two. No one seems to know the complete story or who managed the massive undertaking, as it must have been. According to an old article in *The Arizona Republic*, the "I" alone is a 100 feet tall and 12 feet wide. To get there, head east on U.S. 60 toward Apache Junction. Take Loop 202 north toward McDowell Road; exit at Hawes Road, and take

The Maricopa County Parks System has 13 parks, including Usery Mountain Regional Park.

The Phoenix arrow has pointed the way since the 1950s.

Hawes Road north to Usery Pass Road. As you travel northeast along Usery Pass Road, look over to your left and you'll see the Phoenix Arrow pointing west.

THE PHOENIX ARROW

WHAT A giant sign

WHERE Usery Pass Road

COST Free

PRO TIP Several west-facing campgrounds and hiking trails in Usery Mountain Regional Park offer excellent views of the Phoenix Arrow.

84

TEMPE'S BRIDGE TO NOWHERE

Why is there only part of a bridge still standing in Tempe?

Tempe, originally settled as Hayden's Ferry during the late 19th century, was established as a ferry crossing. Throughout the Valley's growth explosion during the 20th century, Tempe continued to serve as one of three key crossings, especially when heavy rains fell and the Salt River overran its banks. At one time, two main bridges crossed the Salt River near what is now known as Tempe Town Lake. The old, old bridge built between 1911 and 1913 originally handled mostly pedestrian traffic, and a "newer" automobile bridge was built in 1931. The original Old Tempe Bridge, also known as the State Street Bridge and the Old Ash Avenue Bridge, was considered highly advanced at the time and became one of the state's early historic structures. In the late 1970s, the Valley was plagued by a series of floods that sent the Salt River raging across the desert, washing out roads and flooding bridges. At one point, flooding was so bad that people found themselves stranded on one side of the river or the other. The onslaught of water proved too much for the Old Ash Avenue Bridge; the high waters damaged

---

OLD TEMPE BRIDGE

WHAT A bridge monument

WHERE Tempe Town Lake Park

COST Free

PRO TIP Climb the stairs to the top of the monument for a better view of Tempe and the lake.

Top: The old bridge provides an elevated view of Tempe.
Right: The old Ash Avenue Bridge abutment.

it beyond repair. It remained standing for another 10 years until engineers and architects convinced the city that it was unsafe even for pedestrian traffic. The Old Ash Avenue Bridge abutment, which sits on the south side of the lake, remains as a monument to what was once a historic and innovative bridge. Today, the old Tempe Bridge is the Old Mill Avenue Bridge built in 1931. It carries southbound car, bicycle, and pedestrian traffic into Downtown Tempe. The newer Mill Avenue Bridge, which opened in 1993, carries northbound traffic across the lake to Papago Park.

According to local papers, the Old Mill Avenue Bridge built in 1931 was considered the "grand old lady."

85

THE COUNTRY'S BIGGEST UFO SIGHTING

Did the Phoenix Lights really happen?

The country's biggest UFO sighting did not happen in Roswell. It happened in Phoenix, Arizona. According to thousands of witnesses, an unidentified flying object, otherwise known as a UFO, made its way across the night skies above Arizona on March 13, 1997. The V-shaped aircraft left a 300-mile swath of confused individuals in its wake, including Arizona's governor at the time, Fife Symington. The incident not only made the local news; it also captured nationwide interest when the story landed in the pages of *USA Today* a few months later.

No one claims that the event didn't happen, but some are still scrambling to explain it. The military claims to this day that it was part of a training operation over the Gila River, but many who witnessed the event claim that it couldn't have been a group of American-made aircraft, or the flares they supposedly dropped. In fact, most witnesses claim it was a single, massive, boomerang-shaped craft that passed quietly overhead, leaving them speechless, and in some cases, a little dazed. Part of the mystery of the Phoenix Lights is that so many people witnessed it. Several even captured the experience on video. The other part is that, like any good conspiracy, it has yet to be explained.

Today, it is considered one of the most visible UFO encounters of all time.

Downtown Phoenix skyline.

PHOENIX LIGHTS

WHAT "UFO" encounter

PRO TIP Every year on the anniversary local news stories pop up.

86 THE NOT SO GREAT PAPAGO ESCAPE

Did German POWs make it down the Gila River to Mexico?

Papago Park was once home to a World War II prisoner-of-war camp. Built in 1943, the camp became home to somewhere between 3,000 and 5,000 German soldiers. (There was also a camp at the park for Italian prisoners of war, but they were held separately.) Most of the prisoners were naval personnel who were captured by the British. The prisoners were required to help in the cotton fields, and both German and Italian POWs attempted several escapes, the largest of which was made on the day before Christmas 1944. Led by a U-boat captain, 25 German soldiers made their way through a 200-foot dirt tunnel to freedom. Apparently, their plan was to take the Salt River to the Gila River and float their way into Mexico. Stymied by the Salt River's lack of water, one was picked up outside the camp, and five of the escapees were "rescued" on the shores of the Salt River. They claimed they needed food, but their packs were full. Perhaps they were too embarrassed to admit they didn't want to walk to the Mexico border almost 200 miles to the south. The remaining 19 prisoners made various attempts to get to Mexico on foot, with a handful getting as far as 25

PAPAGO PARK POW CAMP

WHAT A not so great escape

WHERE Papago Park, Phoenix, Arizona

COST Free

PRO TIP The Sports Complex on 64th Street and McDowell Road is at the site of the old POW camp.

Top: Papago Park, where the POW camp was located.
Left: The trickle of the Salt River did little to aid the escape.

miles from the border. The last of them, the captain who led the escape, was picked up almost a month later in downtown Phoenix. The local story is that the Germans had attempted to ride the Salt River south to Mexico. As you can imagine, even in a rainstorm, the river wouldn't carry them very far or for very long.

The POW escape is said to be
the largest in U.S. history.
Fortunately, it was not a successful one.

87

THE SONORAN DESERT'S MIGHTY SENTINELS

What are those giant green things?

Those towering sentinels marching across the desert and up the mountainsides would be cactus—the saguaro cactus to be exact, and the Sonoran Desert, which covers southern Arizona and the western part of Sonora, Mexico, is the only place in the world where you'll find them. This desert giant is said to grow as tall as 40 to 60 feet and can have as many as 25 arms (those curved limbs growing out of its sides). They grow very slowly and can live to be 200 years old. The best place to see the saguaro is in its natural habitat—the desert. You'll find pockets of desert sprinkled throughout the city: Papago Park and South Mountain Park Preserve in Phoenix as well as Usery

---

SAGUARO CACTUS

WHAT Arizona's most well-known icon

WHERE Everywhere across the Valley

COST Free

PRO TIP Such nearby lakes as Lake Pleasant and Canyon Lake offer a unique view of the undulating, saguaro-studded mountainsides.

Top: The many-armed saguaro cactus at Usery Mountain Regional Park.
Right: The ribs of a dead saguaro cactus.

Mountain Regional Park in Mesa and the McDowell Mountains in Scottsdale and Fountain Hills. Arizona is very protective of its most recognizable icon. In fact, according to the Arizona State Legislature website, Arizona Revised Statute 3-932 makes it a class 4 felony to remove or destroy native plants (including the saguaro cactus) from private or state land.

The saguaro blossom is Arizona's state flower and only blooms at night, usually in late spring/early summer.

88

GIANT IN THE SKY

What is that giant thing hanging along Central Avenue?

"What is it?" That's the question people usually ask when they see the public art piece *Her Secret Is Patience*. swaying gently, high above Civic Space Park on Central Avenue between Polk and Fillmore, the 145-foot-tall aerial sculpture was inspired by several things—all of them an integral part of the desert—fossils, monsoon clouds, and cacti. Designed by artist Janet Echelman and installed in 2009, the stunning piece at the very least gives pause and at the most encourages contemplation. It most often inspires viewers to look up, which was Echelman's intention. The movement of the sculpture creates shapes and shadows on the ground during the day and at night shifts through the cool colors of winter or the warm colors of summer. Echelman chose the colors to present at opposite times of year—cooling Phoenix parkgoers in the summer and warming them in the winter. The installment of the $2 million piece was a collaboration by a team of artists, architects, designers, fabricators, and engineers.

Civic Space Park is part of ASU's downtown Phoenix campus. At just under three acres, the green space is not large but is centrally located. The park has been known to host events and even morning yoga sessions.

Echelman is known for her larger-than-life sculptures that, like *Her Secret Is Patience*, blend movement and light.

Her Secret Is Patience *hangs suspended above Civic Space Park near the light rail.*

HER SECRET IS PATIENCE

WHAT Public art

WHERE 424 N. Central Ave., Phoenix, Arizona

COST Free

PRO TIP At night, the structure is a colorful display of light.

197

89 ON THE SHOULDERS OF GIANTS

Why is there a dancing pickle on the side of that building?

Situated in a mostly Hispanic neighborhood east of central Phoenix, the Arnold pickle catches your eye as you head east on Van Buren Avenue. Painted on the west wall of an old red brick building on 14th Avenue, it serves as a reminder of the family-owned businesses that have grown up in Phoenix during the last century.

The A Pickle House was started by pioneers William and Bessie Arnold in 1905. The couple started out selling pickles door to door, and in true pioneer spirit they soon built a burgeoning brand that would someday become a household name. At one time, the Arnold Pickle & Olive Co. (as it was renamed) was one of the largest privately owned businesses of its kind in the Southwest. The brand was eventually acquired by Green Bay Foods, a large, Wisconsin-based food distributor. Even after they sold the rights to the brand, the Arnold family continued to operate their business in the same location under a new name until 1989. The white-and-black sign that still hangs out front is connected with another Arnold Family business—rustic furniture. One of the Arnolds' descendants converted the old leftover equipment and cabinetry into furniture.

The sign you see today was updated in 1996 to preserve the Arnold Pickle House name.

198

The dancing pickle at the Arnold Pickle House.

The property stayed in the family into the 1990s and was eventually purchased by the local nonprofit Chicanos Por La Causa. In 2014, a $3 million grant was awarded to the nonprofit. Recent announcements have indicated plans to convert the 35,000-square-foot warehouse into a maker space, capitalizing on the spirit of entrepreneurship steeped in the building's very bricks, just like the briny pickle smell that neighbors once caught a whiff of.

THE PICKLE HOUSE

WHAT Historic building

WHERE 1401 E. Van Buren

COST Free

PRO TIP The word "pickle" is painted on the front of the building.

90 PHOENIX'S FIRST "GREEN" HOUSE

Where is Mystery Castle?

With a name like Mystery Castle, by right, it has to be included in any list of the secret, hidden, and obscure. The existence of the house, built by Boyce Luther Gulley, was once a mystery, but the story of how it came to be has been told time and again by his daughter—Mary Lou Gulley. The "castle" was built for her by her father, but he died before he could share it with her. Mary Lou lived in the home for decades and gave tours to the public, sharing what her father had built more than a half-century before. The five-level castle features 18 rooms and 13 fireplaces and took almost 20 years to build. Every inch of it was handcrafted by a single man from bits and pieces of salvaged brick, concrete, old metal tubs, and wooden wagon wheels—even rocks from the surrounding desert—most of which her father found and hauled back to the homesite.

Boyce Luther Gulley was an amateur architect who left his wife and daughter in Seattle in 1927 to escape the health problems he faced from tuberculosis. He fully expected to die, but he began to feel better after arriving in Phoenix and started creating his castle. Over almost two decades, he designed and assembled

Mystery Castle is on Mineral Road off 7th Street, nestled in the South Mountain Preserve.

Top: *Mystery Castle at South Mountain Preserve.*
Above: *The castle is an amalgamation of salvaged bits and pieces.*

MYSTERY CASTLE

WHAT A father's tribute to his daughter

WHERE The Mystery Castle is located in the foothills of South Mountain Park (two miles south of Baseline Road) at 800 E. Mineral Rd. in Phoenix, Arizona.

COST $10 per adult

PRO TIP Spring, winter, and fall are the best times for a tour. The castle is not air-conditioned.

the house, only stopping in 1945 when he died. A year later his daughter, Mary Lou, arrived in Phoenix to see the mysterious home her father had bequeathed in his will.

Upon her death in 2010, a foundation was formed to preserve the home and continue her tradition of giving tours and sharing the story of her castle in the desert.

<u>91</u> QUIET GROVE IN THE CITY

Why is there a pecan grove in the middle of the city?

The Farm at South Mountain is a remnant of the city's earlier agricultural days. The entire area is a hodgepodge of apartment buildings; older homes; long, narrow lots with gardens and greenhouses; goats, chickens, horses, donkeys, and even sheep; a small ranch; a timeshare; and two championship golf courses. Those long, narrow garden-laden lots were part of Dwight Heard's (of the Heard Museum and the Heard Building) vision for "a sustainable future." Heard was a very forward-thinking man for the early 20th century, and he picked an ideal spot to begin parceling out property. The 10-acre pecan grove, which sits just north of the South Mountain Park Preserve only minutes from downtown Phoenix, was

The Farm at South Mountain.

also part of his vision. Today, it is nestled between an empty lot and private property and offers a quiet place in the middle of the bustling urban core of South Phoenix. The Farm is now owned and operated by local chef Pat Christofolo. Her three restaurants serve a combination of breakfast, lunch, and/or dinner. The Farm's

Chef Dustin Christofolo was invited to bring his Arizona cuisine to the James Beard House in Manhattan in 2016.

Top: Picnic tables in the pecan grove.
Above: The businesses at The Farm.

THE FARM AT SOUTH MOUNTAIN

WHAT An old pecan grove

WHERE 6106 S. 32nd St., Phoenix, Arizona

COST The cost of a meal

PRO TIP If you plan to eat at Quiessence, make reservations. They only serve dinner.

on-site farm supplies seasonal produce and herbs to each of the restaurants, redefining farm to table as a way of life.

Three restaurants can be found at The Farm at South Mountain: Morning Glory Cafe, the Farm Kitchen, and Quiessence. There is also a store named Botanica, which features handcrafted items, including home decor, soaps, and candles, and the property offers various events, such as a Mother's Day Brunch, and educational opportunities, such as cooking classes and aromatherapy workshops. Tucked far back on the property is the crown jewel of the farm—Quiessence. Managed by Pat's son, Chef Dustin Christofolo, Quiessence elevates the seasonal bounty the farm produces into an Arizona culinary experience.

92 THE SMELL OF WET DESERT

What makes the desert smell that way when it rains?

That distinct desert aroma you smell after it has rained is the scent of the creosote bush. Apparently, when the plant gets wet its oils activate, emitting a woody, camphor smell that you might find similar to pine or rosemary. You may also catch a whiff of it before the rain begins to fall because creosote bushes elsewhere have already gotten wet. For this reason, the creosote fragrance is also a harbinger of rain to come. These hardy plants grow abundantly in most of North America's deserts, including the Sonoran Desert, and are considered the oldest plants alive. Some have been found to be more than 10,000 years old. Cup your hands around the tiny branches of a creosote bush, and blow on it (as if to warm your hands). You'll catch a whiff of that delightful desert-after-the-rain smell. How do you know it's a creosote bush? The plant has gnarled branches and tiny pale green leaves. Several times a year the creosote also puts out small yellow blossoms. In Arizona, creosote is also known as greasewood, a name you may still find across the region, including the town of Greasewood in Navajo County.

Rosemary is another scent you'll smell when it rains heavily in Phoenix.

The creosote bush in spring.

CREOSOTE BUSH

WHAT A plant

WHERE Sonoran Desert

COST Free

PRO TIP You can find these bushes growing along most hiking trails in the Phoenix area.

205

93 THE GUARDIANS OF OLD CITY HALL

Who are those old birds?

Once upon a time in 1928, Old City Hall was known as New City Hall. The H-shaped building, known as the Maricopa County Courthouse, was designed by Louisiana architect Edward F. Neild to house both Phoenix City Hall and the Maricopa County Courthouse. Neild used the Art Deco style of the time and incorporated several uniquely Southwestern effects, including a terra-cotta finish and Native American designs in the building's exterior architecture. The building has many notable features, including the cupola at the top of the building, which once served as the police department's jail, but one of the most stunning aspects of the structure is the west wing entrance, where two magnificent phoenix birds stand guard. Carved into opposite corners of the stone entry, two phoenixes rise from the flames. Between them are the words "Phoenix City Hall." For decades, the west wing was home to the city's municipal offices, including the police department. In 1975, the police department moved out, and in the early 1990s, the city recognized

---

Historic City Hall was dedicated on October 21, 1929, which happened to be a very important day. It was the 50th anniversary of Thomas Edison's invention of the lightbulb.

Phoenix birds continue to guard the entrance to Old City Hall.

a need for a larger city hall; a new one was built in 1993. The west wing of the city-county building became known as Historic or Old City Hall. Today, the building is known as the Maricopa County Courthouse. It houses the Superior Court of Maricopa County and the Phoenix Police Department Museum in the west wing.

OLD CITY HALL

WHAT A historic entrance

WHERE 125 W. Washington St., Phoenix, Arizona

COST Free

PRO TIP Metered parking is available along Jefferson and Washington Streets between First and Third Avenues.

PHOENIX'S OLDEST CEMETERY

Are those headstones in the middle of the city?

In 1914, the City of Phoenix determined that cemeteries could no longer be located within city limits. For that reason, Pioneer & Military Memorial Park is the only place where you'll see headstones in central Phoenix. Just minutes from downtown, the 11-acre park is not a single cemetery, but a combination of seven separate cemeteries with headstones dating

The Smurthwaite House holds the cemetery's burial records.

as far back as 1879. The engraved markers signify the final resting place for some of the famous and infamous characters from Phoenix history. Among the most notable is probably Jacob Waltz of the Legend of the Lost Dutchman's Gold. The pioneer family names represent a multitude of cultures, and the park has been known to host various

"Lord" Darrell Duppa, credited with giving Phoenix its name, is buried here, and his adobe brick home still stands about a mile and a half away at 116 W. Sherman Street.

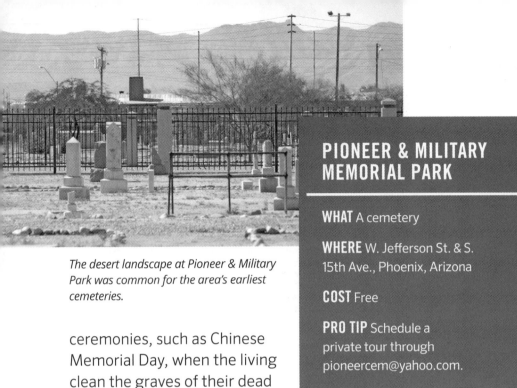

The desert landscape at Pioneer & Military Park was common for the area's earliest cemeteries.

ceremonies, such as Chinese Memorial Day, when the living clean the graves of their dead ancestors, and events, such as the Blarney Stone Open House, which highlights the funeral and wake practices of the Irish, and the Dining among the Dead fund-raiser, hosted by the Pioneers' Cemetery Association in the cemetery's courtyard.

The historic home at the park is the Smurthwaite House. Built in 1897, it was originally located at 602 North Seventh Street. The structure was moved in 1994 to its current location and is home to the Pioneers' Cemetery Association, which manages Pioneer & Military Memorial Park and its burial records. The cemetery's history is layers deep, and archaeological digs and excavations have not only discovered lost graves but also the remains of an old Hohokam village.

The courtyard serves as an outdoor event site in spring, fall, and winter.

BIBLIOGRAPHY

1. **Date Shake**: "The Mysterious Date Palms of Phoenix" *The Arizona Republic*. December 22, 2010. By Niki D'Andrea. http://www.phoenixnewtimes.com/arts/the-mysterious-date-palms-of-phoenix-6582888; "Black Sphinx Dates Arizona" *Sphinx Date Ranch*. http://www.sphinxdateranch.com/black-sphinx-dates-arizona-12oz
2. **Hunt's Tomb**: "Hunt's Tomb" *Phoenix New Times*. July 15, 2010. By Niki D'Andrea. http://www.phoenixnewtimes.com/arts/hunts-tomb-656911; "End Quiet for Noted Executive; Death Takes G.W.P Hunt" *The Arizona Republic*. December 25, 1934. By Ralph O. Brown. http://azcentral.newspapers.com/image/116950311/?terms=hunt%27s%2Btomb
3. **Church of Scientology**: "Ribbon Falls on Ideal Org in the Birthplace of Scientology" *Scientology Today*. June 23, 2012. http://www.scientology.org/scientology-today/church-openings/grand-opening-scientology-ideal-organization-phoenix-arizona.html; "A Slice of Scientology History – Phoenix, Birthplace of the Religion" *Scientology Newsroom*. May 23, 2016. http://www.scientologynews.org/press-releases/a-slice-of-scientology-history-phoenix-birthplace-of-the-religion.html; "L. Ron Hubbard" *Church of Scientology International*. http://www.lronhubbard.org/heritage-sites/phoenix.html; "L. Ron Hubbard's House on 44th Street" *Phoenix New Times*. December 1, 2010. By Niki D'Andrea. http://www.phoenixnewtimes.com/arts/l-ron-hubbards-house-on-44th-street-6578674; "Phoenix Theatre Timeline" *The Arizona Republic*. August 15, 2010. http://archive.azcentral.com/thingstodo/stage/articles/20100815phoenixtheatre0815timeline.html#ixzz4akQnNIea
4. **The Ostrich**: "The Ostrich" *Crust Restaurants*. http://crustrestaurants.com/ostrich/; "The Ostrich Opens in Downtown Chandler, Serving Speakeasy Classics" *Phoenix New Times*. November 18, 2015. By Shelby Moore. http://www.phoenixnewtimes.com/restaurants/the-ostrich-opens-in-downtown-chandler-serving-speakeasy-classics-7777325; "100-Year-Old Basement's Speakeasy Legend Gains New Life in Chandler" *The Arizona Republic*. May 31, 2016. By Chris Coppola. http://www.azcentral.com/story/news/local/chandler/2015/05/31/year-old-basements-speakeasy-legend-gains-new-life-chandler/28089585/
5. **Arabian Horse Show**: "Scottsdale Arabian Horse Show" *Arabian Horse Association of Arizona*. http://www.scottsdaleshow.com/shows-events/scottsdale-arabian-horse-show; "Westworld" *Westworld of Scottsdale*. http://www.westworldaz.com; "Horseworld" *Scottsdale Public Art*. http://www.scottsdalepublicart.org/permanent-art/horseworld
6. **South Mountain Park Preserve**: "South Mountain Park/Preserve" *City of Phoenix*. https://www.phoenix.gov/parks/trails/locations/south-mountain
7. **Frank Lloyd Wright**: "Buildings by Southwest Region" *Frank Lloyd Wright Foundation*. http://franklloydwright.org/; "History-ASU Gammage From the Beginning" *ASU Gammage*. http://www.asugammage.com/about/history
8. **Buckhorn Baths**: "Throwback Thursday: Mesa's Buckhorn Baths' Future" *The Arizona Republic*. January 8, 2016. By Jay Mark. http://www.azcentral.com/story/news/local/mesa/contributor/2016/01/08/throwback-thursday-mesas-buckhorn-baths-future/78109056/; "Buckhorn Mineral Baths advertisement" *The Arizona Republic*. November 22, 1942. http://azcentral.newspapers.com/image/117318854/?terms=%22buckhorn%2Bbaths%22
9. **The Lost Dutchman's Gold**: "The Legend of the Lost Dutchman Mine" *Lost Dutchman Days*. http://www.lostdutchmandays.org/legend.htm; "Has the Lost Dutchman Mine Been Found? A team of researchers is on the prowl for Jacob Waltz's treasure." *True West Magazine*. April 1, 2005. By Bob Willis. http://www.truewestmagazine.com/has-the-lost-dutchman-mine-been-found/; "Lost Dutchman Gold Mine: Does 'X' mark the spot?" *The Huffington Post*. March 14, 2015. By Lee Speigel. http://www.huffingtonpost.com/2015/03/14/superstition-mountains-lost-dutchman-gold-mine_n_6835264.html
10. **Orpheum Theater**: "New Orpheum Theater, Costing $750,000, Last Word In Playhouse Construction; Opening Date is Announced for Saturday" *The Arizona Republic*. December 30, 1928; "New Orpheum, Arizona's Finest Theater, Will Be Formerly Opened January 5; Building here is erected at $750,000 cost" *The Arizona Republic*. December 28, 1928.
11. **Petroglyphs**: "Hohokam Petroglyphs at South Mountain Park" *Phoenix New Times*. August 11, 2010. By Niki D'Andrea. http://www.phoenixnewtimes.com/arts/hohokam-petroglyphs-at-south-mountain-park-6557466
12. **Pizza**: "These Are the Cities With America's Favorite Pizza 2016" *Travel and Leisure*. February 3, 2017. By Megan Soll. http://www.travelandleisure.com/americas-favorite-places/best-cities-for-pizza#bazbeaux-indianapolis-pizz-trio; "Phoenix Named America's

Best Pizza City by Travel + Leisure" *The Arizona Republic*. February 7, 2017. By Jennifer McClellan. http://www.azcentral.com/story/entertainment/dining/2017/02/07/phoenix-named-americas-best-pizza-city-travel-leisure/97591508/

13. **St. Mary's Basilica**: "Churches" *GCatholic*. http://www.gcatholic.org/churches/data/basUS.htm; "Basilica History" *St. Mary's Basilica*. http://saintmarysbasilica.org/basilica-history/; "Papal Visit St. Mary's Basilica" *The Arizona Republic*. September 15, 1987; "St. Mary's Was 32nd In U.S. To Be Designated Minor Basilica" *The Arizona Republic*. September 15, 1987. By Mary A.M. Gindhart.

14. **Eisendrath House**: "Rose Eisendrath House" *City of Tempe*. http://www.tempe.gov/city-hall/community-development/historic-preservation/tempe-historic-property-register/rose-eisendrath-house; "Five Southeast Valley Spots Off Beaten History Path" *The Arizona Republic*. November 26, 2014. By Srianthi Perera; "Remodeling Planned For Desert Dwelling" *The Arizona Republic*. July 14, 1940, p15.

15. **Jones-Montoya House**: "State's Earliest Homes Defy Time" *The Arizona Republic*. October 3, 2009. By Peter Corbett. http://archive.azcentral.com/style/hfe/decor/articles/2009/10/03/20091003oldhomes.html; "Swift Action is Required at Jones-Montoya House" *The Arizona Republic*. December 7, 2013. By Dustin Gardiner.

16. **Virginia C. Piper**: "Virginia G. Piper Biography" *Piper Trust*. http://pipertrust.org/VirginiaPiperBiography/chapter_05_06.html

17. **Secret Room at Four Peaks**: "The Closing of Uranus Recording Marks End of Era for a Gin Blossom" *Phoenix New Times*. July 15, 2015. http://www.phoenixnewtimes.com/music/the-closing-of-uranus-recording-marks-end-of-era-for-a-gin-blossom-7488477; Four Peaks Culture. https://www.fourpeaks.com/culture/

18. **The Miranda Warning**: "Miranda Legal Case Unique" *The Arizona Republic*. June 29, 1966. By James Marlow; "Phoenix 101: The Deuce" *The Rogue Columnist*. May 9, 2011. By Jon Talton. http://www.roguecolumnist.com/rogue_columnist/2011/05/phoenix-101-the-deuce.html

19. **Steven Spielberg**: "AZ Insider: Spielberg Makes Music with Symphonies" *Arizona Foothills Magazine*. September 2013. By Kathy Shayna Shocket. http://www.arizonafoothillsmagazine.com/the-az-insider/5915-az-insider.html; "Close Encounters of the Steven Spielberg Kind in Arizona" *Forward.com*. April 23, 2015. By Anna Goldenberg. http://forward.com/culture/305981/close-encounters-of-the-arizona-kind/; "Phoenix Theatre Timeline" *The Arizona Republic*. August 15, 2010. http://archive.azcentral.com/thingstodo/stage/articles/20100815phoenixtheatre0815timeline.html

20. **Camels in the Desert**: "Camels Are Part of Arizona History" *KJAZZ*. February 25, 2013. By Nadine Arroyo Rodriguez; "Civil War Spelled End of Wild Camels in Arizona" *USA Today*. February 15, 2011. By Clay Thompson. https://usatoday30.usatoday.com/news/nation/states/arizona/2011-02-15-1042942857_x.htm; "Camelback Mountain" *City of Phoenix*. https://www.phoenix.gov/parks/trails/locations/camelback-mountain

21. **Ostrich Craze**: "Ostrich Festival" *City of Chandler*. http://www.chandleraz.gov/default.aspx?pageid=159; "A Brief History of the Chandler Ostrich Festival" *The Arizona Republic*. March 11, 2017. By Jared MacDonald-Evoy. http://www.azcentral.com/story/news/local/chandler/2017/03/10/history-and-protests-over-chandler-ostrich-festival/98502344/

22. **Sonoran Dog**: "9 Best Sonoran-Style Hot Dogs in Metro Phoenix" *Phoenix New Times*. June 24, 2013. By Heather Hoch. http://www.phoenixnewtimes.com/restaurants/9-best-sonoran-style-hot-dogs-in-metro-phoenix-6539231/2; "Food Truck Guide: Nearly 50 savory and sweet food trucks around Phoenix" *The Arizona Republic*. December 8, 2015. By Jennifer McClellan. http://www.azcentral.com/story/entertainment/dining/2015/12/08/food-guide-55-food-trucks-metro-phoenix/76627796/

23. **ASU's Secret Garden**: Dixie Gammage Hall. *Arizona State University*. https://tours.asu.edu/tempe/dixie-gammage-hall

24. **Mormon Temple**: "Mormon Temple Will Be One of Showplaces of Valley When Completed" *The Arizona Republic*. September 2, 1923, p9. By Sol A. Sprague; "See Stars Tonight as Displays Light Up" *The Arizona Republic*. November 28, 1998.

25. **Phoenix Financial Center**: "The Phoenix Financial Center a.k.a. Western Savings and Loan" *Modern Phoenix*. 2011. By Alison King. http://www.modernphoenix.net/phoenixfinancial.htm; "Center Dedication Ceremony" *The Arizona Republic*. September 27, 1964. By A. V. Gullette.

26. **Enchanted Island**: "Enchanted Island" http://www.enchantedisland.com/; "Encanto Park" *City of Phoenix*. https://www.phoenix.gov/parks/parks/alphabetical/e-parks/encanto-park

27. **Grand Avenue**: "History" *Grand Avenue Arts & Preservation*. By Beatrice Moore and Tony Zahn. http://www.grandavenueartsandpreservation.org/; "10 Changes Coming to the Grand Avenue Arts District in 2016" *Phoenix New Times*. January 18, 2016. By Lynn Trimble. http://www.phoenixnewtimes.com/

arts/10-changes-coming-to-the-grand-avenue-arts-district-in-2016-7973257

28. **The Copper Dome**: "Arizona Capitol Gets Birthday Gift: A shiny new copper dome" *The Arizona Republic*. February 12, 2012. By Mary Jo Pitzl; "Do You Remember? 40 years ago today, Aug 5, 1910" *The Arizona Republic*. August 5, 1950, p6; "Beneath the Copper Dome" *The Arizona Republic*. February 10, 2002, p104. By Belinda Long.

29. **Stockyards**: "History" *Stockyards Steakhouse*. http://www.stockyardssteakhouse. com/history.html; "Family's Office Plan to Revive Stockyards Restaurant" *The Business Journal*. June 1, 2003. By Mike Padgett. http://www.bizjournals.com/phoenix/ stories/2003/06/02/story4.html; "Stockyards to be Preserved; Jokake set to renovate historic restaurant" *The Arizona Republic*. October 11, 2003, p284. By Mike Fimea.

30. **Hashknife Pony Express**: "Posse Making Trek to Phoenix Rodeo" *The Arizona Republic*. March 3, 1959, p17; "Hashknife Riders Bringing Letter; Pony Express lives again in Arizona" *The Arizona Republic*. March 10, 1959; "Running a Pony Express" *The Arizona Republic*. May 26, 1892, p2; "Pony Express Historical Timeline" *Pony Express National Museum*. http://ponyexpress.org/pony-express-historical-timeline/

31. **Tovrea Castle**: "Tovrea Castle" *Arizona PBS*. http://www.azpbs.org/arizonastories/ seasontwo/tovreacastle.htm

32. **Salt River**: No sources.

33. Hidden Haunts: "The Spirit of Casey Moore's" Casey Moore's. http://www.caseymoores. com/; "*Ghost Hunting* at Casey Moore's" *Phoenix New Times*. October 30, 2008. By Martin Cizmar and Kelly Wilson. http://www.phoenixnewtimes.com/music/ghost-hunting-at-casey-moores-6609013; "Phoenix Hotel's "Ghosts" Star on Travel Channel" *The Arizona Republic*. January 17, 2004. By Angela Cara Pancrazio; "Hobgoblin Hotel" *The Arizona Republic*. October 26, 1998, By Thomas Ropp; "Woman Takes Own Life by Seven-Story Leap From Hotel San Carlos" *The Arizona Republic*. May 8, 1928.

34. **Weather**: "Republic Special Report: See What's Behind Arizona's Dust Storms" The Arizona Republic. July 24, 2011; "Haboobs Hit Phoenix" The Arizona Republic. February 25, 1973. By Mary Leonhard.

35. **George Washington Carver Museum**: "Old-School Ways" *Phoenix New Times*. May 30, 1996. By Terry Greene Sterling. *http*://www.phoenixnewtimes.com/news/old-school-ways-6423931; "Phoenix School That Was Segregated Envisioned As 'A Place You Can Talk the Truth'" *The Arizona Republic*. January 25, 2017. By Brenna Goth. *http://ww*w.azcentral. com/story/news/local/phoenix/2017/01/25/segregated-phoenix-george-washington-carver-high-school-envisioned-museum/95349730/

36. **Sandra Day O'Connor House**: "Arizona Judge Becomes First Woman Nominated for Supreme Court Post" The Arizona Republic. July 8,1981; "Good Appointment" The Arizona Republic. October 28, 1969; "Judge O'Connor Earned Peers' Respect" The Arizona Republic. July 8, 1981. By Chuck Hawley; "Sandra Day O'Connor House" *City of Tempe*. http://www.tempe.gov/city-hall/community-development/historic-preservation/ tempe-historic-property-register/sandra-day-o-connor-house

37. **Rattlesnake**: No sources.

38. **Japanese Internment Camps**: "Statement of Policy Text on the Treatment of Japanese" *The Arizona Republic*. July 18, 1943; "More Than 16,000 Individuals – Women, Men and Children – Were Relocated to Gila River Internment Camp Only a Few Miles Away From Chandler" *City of Chandler*. http://www.chandleraz.gov/default.aspx?pageid=1003; "Executive Order No. 9066" *City of Chandler*. http://www.chandleraz.gov/content/PC%20UnAmerican%20 2017%20WEB%20020817.pdf; "Japanese Internments: Righting an injustice" *The Arizona Republic*. August 6, 1988, p24; "Mesa History: Japanese internment and the Mesa experience" *The Arizona Republic*. January 12, 2017. By Jay Mark.

39. **Peacocks at Sahuaro Ranch**: "Flock a Feathered Legacy; Sahuaro Ranch home for decades to peacock family" *The Arizona Republic*. September 8, 2004, p96. By Paula Hubbs Cohen.

40. **Hotel Valley Ho**: "A Mid-Century Modern Star is Born - Hotel Valley Ho" *Historic Hotels of America*.http://m.historichotels.org/basicphone/index.php/property/history?id=hotel-valley-ho; "World's Coolest Pools" *Travel + Leisure*. By Jimmy Im. http://www. travelandleisure.com/slideshows/worlds-coolest-pools/9

41. **Marston**: "3-D Astronomy Shows" *ASU-School of Earth and Space Exploration*. https:// sese.asu.edu/public-engagement/3-d-astronomy

42. **Fountain Hills**: "McColloch Reveals Plans of New "City": Will spend $100 million in five years on community near Scottsdale" *The Arizona Republic*. By Clyde A. Murray; "Fun Facts and History of Fountain Hills" *Sonoran Lifestyle Real Estate*. http://sonoranlifestyle.com/ fun-facts-history-of-fountain-hills/

43. **Carefree Highway**: "Carefree Highway" *GordonLightfoot.com*. http://www. gordonlightfoot.com/carefreehighway.shtml

44. **Piestewa Peak**: "Piestewa Hiking Trail Map and Descriptions" *City of Phoenix*. https://www.

phoenix.gov/parks/trails/locations/piestewa-peak/hiking-trail-map; "Lori Piestewa: The Story of a Brave Soldier" *U.S. Army*. https://www.army.mil/americanindians/piestewa. html; "Phoenix Adds Signs for Piestewa Peak Amid Street Name Controversy" *The Arizona Republic*. April 5, 2017. By Dustin Gardiner. http://www.azcentral.com/story/news/local/ phoenix/2017/04/05/phoenix-adds-signs-piestewa-peak-amid-squaw-peak-drive-street-name-controversy/99887556/

45. **Phoenix-Mesa Gateway**: "T-38A Talon - Phoenix-Mesa Gateway Airport, Mesa, AZ" *Groundspeak*. http://www.waymarking.com/waymarks/WM98C4_T_38A_Talon_ Phoenix_Mesa_Gateway_Airport_Mesa_AZ; "Air Combat" *Fighter Combat International*. https://fightercombat.com/air-combat/; "Facility" *Air Combat International*. https:// fightercombat.com/why-us/facility-office-hangar; "About Gateway" *Phoenix-Mesa Gateway Airport*. http://www.gatewayairport.com/aboutgateway.aspx

46. **Papago Park**: "Papago Park" *City of Phoenix*. https://www.phoenix.gov/parks/trails/ locations/papago-park

47. **Wrigley Mansion Club**: "Wrigley Mansion Should Be Open to Everyone" *The Arizona Republic*. March 13, 1988. By Celeste Nichols; "Wrigley Mansion's New Wine Bar: Very dark, very sultry, sexy and chic." *The Arizona Republic*. November 4, 2016. By Gwen Ashley Walters. http://www.azcentral.com/story/entertainment/dining/2016/11/04/ wrigley-mansions-new-wine-bar/92915780/

48. **Mystery Room**: "Arizona Biltmore Press Release" http://www.arizonabiltmore.com/ wp-content/uploads/2015/01/Latest-News-at-the-Biltmore.pdf

49. **Luhrs Tower**: "Luhrs Family Reminisces About Historic Downtown Phoenix Buildings" *Phoenix Business Journal*. March 2, 2015. By Hayley Ringle. http://www.bizjournals.com/ phoenix/blog/techflash/2015/03/luhrs-family-reminisces-downtown-phoenix.html; "Structure Will Be At First and Jefferson" *The Arizona Republic*. November 4, 1928; "High-Rise Trio Hit Downtown Drawing Board" *The Arizona Republic*. August 13, 2014. By Betty Reid.

50. **Sun Devils**: "Sparky" *Sun Devil Athletics*. http://www.thesundevils.com/ sports/2013/4/17/208256866.aspx; "History" *Arizona State University*. http://www.asu. edu/asuweb/about/history/

51. **Amtrak**: "It's the End of the Line: Firm eyes leasing train station as Amtrak weighs pull out" *The Arizona Republic*. July 31, 1995. By Mike Padgett; "Dream on Track; Tempe rail service attracting interest" *The Arizona Republic*. August 17, 1983, By Cathryn R. Shaffer; "Phoenix Arizona (PHX)" *Train Web*. http://www.trainweb.org/usarail/phoenix.htm

52. **Don Bolles**: "My Turn: Reporter Don Bolles was killed for telling the truth" *The Arizona Republic*. May 28, 2016. By John Winters. http://www.azcentral.com/story/opinion/ op-ed/2016/05/29/don-bolles/84878980/; "Shadowy Mob Became Target of Bolles' Reporting. *The Arizona Republic*. June 3, 1976, p6. By Connie Koenenn; "Fake Tipster Lured Writer, Police Believe" *The Arizona Republic*. June 3, 1976, p1. By Jack West and Earl Zarbin; "'They Finally Got Me', Newsman Cries After Blast" *The Arizona Republic*. June 3, 1976, p1. By Paul Dean.

53. **Cotton Fields**: "Cotton Today" *Arizona Experience*. http://Arizonaexperience.org/land/ cotton-today; "History of Goodyear" *City of Goodyear*. http://Goodyearaz.gov/about-us/ demographics-growth/history-of-goodyear

54. **USS Arizona**: "USS *Arizona*: State will dedicate memorial to lost crewmen" *The Arizona Republic*. December 5, 1976. By John L. Schwartz.

55. **Peterson House**: "Windows on History; Hotel renovation part of Chandler project" *The Arizona Republic*. August 14, 1999, p177. By Melissa L. Jones; "Niels Petersen House" *City of Tempe*. http://www.tempe.gov/city-hall/community-development/historic-preservation/ tempe-historic-property-register/niels-petersen-house

56. **Canals**: "Lifeblood of Phoenix: 7 things to know about canals" *The Arizona Republic*. January 20, 2017. By Dustin Gardiner. http://azcentral.com/story/news/local/ phoenix/2017/01/20/phoenix-canals-history-7-things-to-know/96695158; "Canal History" *Salt River Project*. https://www.srpnet.com/water/canals/history.aspx

57. **Durant's Front Door**: "Separating Legend of Jack Durant and His Steak House From Movie Myths" *The Arizona Republic*. January 20, 2016. By Richard Ruelas. http://www.azcentral. com/story/entertainment/movies/2016/01/20/jack-durant-movie-myths/78324520/; "15 Fun Facts About Durant's Steakhouse in Phoenix" *The Arizona Republic*. July 30, 2014. By Kylie Gad. http://www.azcentral.com/story/entertainment/dining/2014/07/30/ durants-phoenix-steakhouse-history-fun-facts/13288547/

58. **Indian Reservations**: "Fact Check: Gosar correct on private land in Arizona" *The Arizona Republic*. April 13, 2015. By Julia Shumway. http:// www.azcentral.com/story/news/politics/fact-check/2015/04/13/ fact-check-gosar-correct-private-land-arizona/25740527/

59. **Falcon Field**: "Name of Field Will Be Falcon" *The Arizona Republic*. July 31, 1941; "Falcon Field in Mesa Offering Air Tours in WWII Planes" *The Arizona Republic*. November 7, 2014. By Mark Nothaft. http://www.azcentral.com/story/news/local/mesa/2014/11/07/falcon-field-mesa-air-tours-world-war-ii-bomber-planes/18674559/

60. **Hottest Day on Record**: "Marshall Trimble's Official Arizona Trivia" By Marshall Trimble. *Golden West Publishers*. 3rd printing, 2004; "3 Die in Valley — Today: Only 120-degrees" *Weather.com*. June 27, 1990, pA1 and A14. By Mike Burgess. https://weather.com/forecast/regional/news/death-valley-120-degree-heat; "Forget Snow: Jetliners in Phoenix 'heatbound'" *The Arizona Republic*. June 27, 1990, pA1-2. By Guy Webster. http://www.azcentral.com/story/news/local/arizona/2015/06/24/phoenix-hottest-day-extreme-weather-arizona/29166901/; "Arizona Temp Records Toppled by Deadly Heat Wave" *The Arizona Republic*. June 19, 2016. By Amanda Etchison. http://www.azcentral.com/story/news/local/phoenix-weather/2016/06/19/temperatures-top-daily-record-phoenix-yuma/86118102/; "Hottest Day on Record in AZ" *The Arizona Republic*. June 24, 2015. By Shaun McKinnon. http://www.azcentral.com/story/news/local/arizona/2015/06/24/arizona-real-hottest-day-ever-extreme-weather/29198477/

61. **Phoenix Warehouse District**: "History" *Phoenix Warehouse District*. http://www.phxwd.com/history/

62. **Cattle Track Arts Compound**: "Arts Compound a Little Known Gem" *The Arizona Republic*. September 20, 2009. By Sonja Haller. http://archive.azcentral.com/community/scottsdale/articles/2009/09/10/20090910sr-gncattletrack0920.html; "Arizona Pioneer Seamstress Left Fashion Legacy; 'Cattle Track Couture' on display at arts compound" *The Arizona Republic*. March 26, 2012. By Lois McFarland. http://archive.azcentral.com/community/scottsdale/articles/20120323pioneer-seamstress-left-fashion-legacy.html

63. **Double Butte Cemetery**: "Who's Buried in Tempe Cemeteries?" *The Arizona Republic*. February 18, 2016. http://www.azcentral.com/story/news/local/tempe/2016/02/18/whos-buried-tempe-cemeteries/80460882/; "A History of Tempe's Double Butte Cemetery" *City of Tempe*. 2001. By Cheryl L. Fox. http://www.tempe.gov/home/showdocument?id=46743

64. **Desert Blooms**: No sources.

65. **McDonald's**: "The Business Beat" *The Arizona Republic*. May 6, 1953. By Frank Crehan; "Mac Daddy" *Phoenix Magazine*. August 2016. By Keridwen Cornelius. http://www.phoenixmag.com/history/mac-daddy.html

66. **Monti's**: "Hayden, Carl Trumbull, (1877 - 1972)" *Biographical Directory of the United States Congress*.http://bioguide.congress.gov/scripts/biodisplay.pl?index=H000385; "Tempe's Iconic Monti's La Casa Vieja Closing Nov. 17" *The Arizona Republic*. November 3, 2014. By Amy Edelen. http://www.azcentral.com/story/news/local/tempe/2014/11/03/tempes-iconic-montis-la-casa-vieja-closing-nov/18436845/; "Charles Trumbull Hayden House" *City of Tempe*. http://www.tempe.gov/city-hall/community-development/historic-preservation/tempe-historic-property-register/c-t-hayden-house

67. **Hall of Flame**: "Hall of Flame" *Hall of Flame Museum of Firefighting*. http://www.hallofflame.org

68. **Del Webb's Sun City**: "Del Webb's Retirement of Sun City of 1600 Homes Will Open Today" *The Arizona Republic*. January 1, 1960; "237 Sun City Homes Sold" *The Arizona Republic*. January 4, 1960.

69. **Daylight Saving Time**: "Del Webb's Retirement of Sun City of 1600 Homes Will Open Today" *The Arizona Republic*. January 1, 1960.

70. **Citrus**: "Citrus" *The Arizona Experience*. http://arizonaexperience.org/land/citrus; "For a Bigger Orange Belt; Opinions of prominent men on the subject" *The Arizona Republic*. January 17, 1909, p15.

71. **Indian School**: "Steele Indian School Park To Be Dedicated" *The Arizona Republic*. November 9, 2001; "Steele Indian School Park" *City of Phoenix*. https://Phoenix.gov/parks/parks/alphabetical/s-parks/steele-indian-school; "Archeology of the Phoenix Indian School" *Archeology Magazine*. March 27, 1998. By Owen Lindauer. https://archive.archeology.com/online/features/phoenix

72. **Grunow Memorial Clinic**: "Phoenix Clinic To Be Unique" *The Arizona Republic*. September 28, 1930, p12; "Did You Know: Grunow Clinic Among The First of Its Kind in Arizona" *KJZZ*. January 9, 2015. By Nadine Arroyo Rodriguez. http://kjzz.org/content/87175/did-you-know-grunow-clinic-among-first-its-kind-arizona

73. **Pueblo Museum**: "Outdoor Trail" *Phoenix Pueblo Museum*. https://www.phoenix.gov/parks/arts-culture-history/pueblo-grande/exhibits/outdoor-ruin-trail

74. **Golden Gate**: "Sadness Tinges Anniversary Celebration of Spanish Church" *The Arizona Republic*. March 4, 1981; "Pioneer in Valley is Image from Past: South Phoenix chooses to spend last years with sky as roof" *The Arizona Republic*. August 19, 1974. By Bonnie

Bartak; "A Vanished Phoenix Barrio: Visions of Life on 16th Street" *Barriozona*. October 15, 2004. By Eduardo Barraza. http://barriozona.com/a-vanished-phoenix-barrio-visions-of-life-on-16th-street/; "Did You Know: Sacred Heart Church Opens Once A Year For Christmas Service" *KJZZ*. December 18, 2015. By Nadine Arroyo Rodriguez. http://kjzz.org/content/240025/did-you-know-sacred-heart-church-opens-once-year-christmas-service

75. **Wallace and Ladmo**: "9 Places That Pay Tribute to 'Wallace and Ladmo'" *The Arizona Republic*. May 30, 2015. By Richard Ruelas. http://www.azcentral.com/story/news/local/arizona/2015/05/31/arizona-places-pay-tribute-wallace-ladmo/28252499/; "Bud Wilkinson, Morning Mayhem: Wallace and Ladmo have popularity in the bag" *The Arizona Republic*. April 1, 1984, p297. http://Wallacewatchers.com

76. **Westward Ho**: "Name Westward Ho Felt Best Symbol of Hostelry's Aim" *The Arizona Republic*. December 15, 1928, p18; "Phoenix's Historic Westward Ho Gets a Makeover" *The Arizona Republic*. August 26, 2016. By Sue Doerfler. http://www.azcentral.com/story/money/real-estate/2015/08/26/westward-ho-historic-property-redevelopment-project/32354003/; "The Westward Ho Miraculously Has Maintained Much of Its Original Splendor and Charm" *Phoenix New Times*. November 24, 2011. http://www.phoenixnewtimes.com/arts/the-westward-ho-miraculously-has-maintained-much-of-its-original-splendor-and-charm-6451392

77. **Code Talkers**: "Sculpture, Words of Praise Salute Navajo 'Code Talkers'" *The Arizona Republic*. March 3, 1989. By Carol Sowers; "A Stone Man All the Way" *The Arizona Republic*. January 10, 2002, pE1. By John Carlos Villani. http://www.lapahie.com/NavajoCodeTalker_Statue_Phoenix.cfm

78. **Lake Pleasant**: "Lake Pleasant History" *Maricopa Parks & Recreation*. http://www.maricopacountyparks.net/park-locator/lake-pleasant-regional-park/park-information/history/; "Don't Get Too Friendly if You Meet a Burro on This Hike" *The Arizona Republic*. March 13, 2017. By Mare Czinar. http://www.azcentral.com/story/travel/arizona/hiking/2017/03/13/lake-pleasant-hike-wild-burro-trail/99148036/; "Plan to Hunt Hundreds of Burros in Mohave County Suspended" *Phoenix New Times*. January 20, 2016. By Miriam Wasser. http://www.phoenixnewtimes.com/news/plan-to-hunt-hundreds-of-burros-in-mohave-county-suspended-7984790

79. **Japanese Gardens**: "The Japanese-American Flower Growers Who Made Phoenix Bloom" *The Arizona Republic*. January 23, 2016. By Kathy Nakagawa. http://www.azcentral.com/story/news/local/phoenix/2016/01/23/japanese-american-flower-growers-who-made-phoenix-bloom/79019904/; "Did You Know: Japanese Flower Gardens Once A South Phoenix Tourist Attraction" *KJZZ*. December 6, 2013. By Nadine Arroyo Rodriguez. http://kjzz.org/content/12425/did-you-know-japanese-flower-gardens-once-south-phoenix-tourist-attraction; "South Mountain Flower Gardens" *A People's Guide to Maricopa County*. April 29, 2011. http://peoplesguidetomaricopa.blogspot.com/2011/04/south-mountain-flower-gardens.html

80. **Indian Fry Bread**: "Frybread" *Smithsonian Magazine*. July 2008, By Jen Miller. http://www.smithsonianmag.com/arts-culture/frybread-79191/; "6 Favorite Sports for Fry Bread Around Metro Phoenix" *Phoenix New Times*. November 19, 2012. By Lauren Saria. http://www.phoenixnewtimes.com/restaurants/6-favorite-spots-for-fry-bread-around-metro-phoenix-6541679/2; "The Fry Bread House Returns to Melrose" *North Central News*. May 2016. By Patty Talahongva. http://northcentralnews.net/2016/dining/the-fry-bread-house-returns-to-melrose/

81. **Agritopia**: "Story/History" *Agritopia*. http://agritopia.com/story-history/

82. **Diving Lady**: "Mesa's Historic Neon 'Diving Lady' Ready To Dive In Again Tuesday Night After $120K Restoration Project, Lights On Starlite Motel Sign Turn Back On" *East Valley Tribune*. April 1, 2013. By Stacie Spring. http://www.eastvalleytribune.com/local/mesa/mesa-s-historic-neon-diving-lady-ready-to-dive-in/article_2968310e-98b7-11e2-854a-001a4bcf887a.html; "The Sign Makers" *The Arizona Republic*. July 22, 2008. By Srianthi Perera. http://archive.azcentral.com/ent/calendar/articles/2008/07/22/20080722neonmakers.html; "Starlite Motel – Mesa, AZ" *Roadside Peek*. By Syd Nagoshi. http://www.roadsidepeek.com/roadusa/southwest/arizona/azmotel/azothermotel/starlitemotel/index.htm

83. **The Phoenix Arrow**: "No Shortage of Adventure in the EV" *The Arizona Republic*. March 8, 2001, p6. By Evelyn Stringham; "Asked and Answered: Straight answer on arrow to Phoenix" *The Arizona Republic*. March 30, 2015. By Andrea Hiland. http://www.azcentral.com/story/news/local/asked-answered/2015/03/31/asked-answered-straight-answer-arrow-phoenix/70707030/

84. **Old Tempe Bridge**: "Ash Avenue Bridge Will Fall in January; City to seek bids to demolish bridge" *The Arizona Republic*. October 10, 1990. By Randy Kull. http://azcentral.newspapers.com/image/122392072/?terms=Ash%2BAvenue%2BBridge%2BWill%2BFa

ll%2Bin%2BJanuary%3B%2BCity%2Bto%2Bseek%2Bbids%2Bto%2Bdemolish%2Bbridge; "Bridge Across the Salt is 'Grand Old Lady'" *The Arizona Republic*. December 25, 1978, p27. By Ann Inskeep. http://azcentral.newspapers.com/image/120195993/?terms=old%2Bte mpe%2Bbridge; "Bridge, Anyone? Tempe will hold big dedication ceremony Saturday" *The Arizona Republic*. February 25, 1994. By Bob Petrie. http://azcentral.newspapers.com/ima ge/123381258/?terms=Tempe%2Bwill%2Bhold%2Bbig%2Bdedication%2Bceremony%2BS aturday

85. **Phoenix Lights**: "The Phoenix Lights: The mystery remains" *CBS5*. March 13, 2014. http://www.cbs5az.com/story/24972073/the-phoenix-lights-the-mystery-remains; "Why Are People Still Talking About the Phoenix Lights?" *The Arizona Republic*. March 11, 2017. https://www.usatoday.com/story/news/local/phoenix/2017/03/11/ why-do-people-still-talk-phoenix-lights-scl/99048730/

86. **POW Camp**: "Nazi Naval Captain Captured in Phoenix" *The Arizona Republic*. January 29, 1945. http://azcentral.newspapers.com/image/117025619/?terms=Papago%2BPark% 2Band%2Bprisoner%2Bof%2Bwar%2Bcamp%2Band%2Bgerman; "Search Underway for Escaped Nazis" *The Arizona Republic*. December 26, 1944. http://azcentral.newspapers. com/image/117291135/?terms=Papago%2BPark%2Band%2Bprisoner%2Bof%2Bwar%2 Bcamp%2Band%2Bgerman; "Rock-Piercing Tunnel Aided Papago Escape" *The Arizona Republic*. December 27, 1944. http://azcentral.newspapers.com/image/117291540/?ter ms=Papago%2BPark%2Band%2Bprisoner%2Bof%2Bwar%2Bcamp%2Band%2Bgerman; "Great Papago Escape: 25 German POWs dug their way out of Phoenix prison camp" *The Arizona Republic*. December 17, 2015. By Roger Naylor. http://www.azcentral.com/story/ travel/2015/12/17/wwii-pows-escape-papago-park-arizona-military-history/77174834/; "Tempe History: When German POWs escaped from Papago Park" *The Arizona Republic*. February 5, 2015. By Jay Mark. http://www.azcentral.com/story/news/local/ mesa/2015/02/05/mesa-history-german-escape-papago-park/22922467/; "Arizona Farmers Get 5,000 War Prisoners" *The Arizona Republic*. October 6, 1943. http://azcentral. newspapers.com/image/117144070/?terms=Papago%2BPark%2Band%2Bprisoner%2 Bof%2Bwar%2Bcamp%2Band%2Bgerman; "Nazis Housed at Park Camp" *The Arizona Republic*. January 7, 1944. http://azcentral.newspapers.com/image/116929272/?terms=P apago%2BPark%2Band%2Bprisoner%2Bof%2Bwar%2Bcamp%2Band%2Bgerman

88. **Her Name is Patience**: "Good Enough Not Good Enough for Phoenix Park" *The Arizona Republic*. August 1, 2007. http://azcentral.newspapers.com/image/126026637/?term s=echelman; "Her Secret Is Patience, Phoenix, AZ, 2009" *Janet Echelman*. http://www. echelman.com/project/her-secret-is-patience/

89. **Pickle House**: "Pickle House Chic" *The Arizona Republic*. June 16, 1999, p225. By Judy Walker. http://azcentral.newspapers.com/search/#query=Pickle+House+Chic; "Business Kept Clan in a Pickle" *The Arizona Republic*. August 7, 1996, p1 and p7. http://azcentral. newspapers.com/image/123612702/?terms=Business%2BKept%2BClan%2Bin%2 Ba%2BPickle; "$3 Million Grant to Transform Pickle House Into 200-Job Incubator in Phoenix" *Phoenix Business Journal*. November 18, 2014. By Angela Gonzales. http://www. bizjournals.com/phoenix/news/2014/11/18/3-million-grant-to-transform-pickle-house-into.html

90. **Mystery Castle**: "Labor of Love: Mystery Castle kept secret until builder died" *The Arizona Republic*. January 28, 1981. http://azcentral.newspapers.com/image/122473761/?terms= Mystery%2BCastle%2Bkept%2Bsecret%2Buntil%2Bbuilder%2Bdied; "My Mystery Castle" *My Mystery Castle*. http://www.mymysterycastle.com/

91. **The Farm at South Main**: "The Farm Story" *The Farm at South Mountain*. https://www. thefarmatsouthmountain.com/the-farm-story/

92. **Creosote Bush**: "What Is That Smell Just Before It Rains? It's eau de desert." *Arizona Republic*. February 10, 2017, p22. By Mark Nothaft. http://www.azcentral.com/story/ news/local/arizona-contributor/2017/02/07/what-smell-before-rains/97561218/; "The Creosote Bush, A Desert Survivor" *Arizona Daily Independent*. March 16, 2014. By Jonathan Duhamel. https://arizonadailyindependent.com/2014/03/16/the-creosote-bush-a-desert-survivor/; "7 Things You Didn't Know About Creosote Bush" *The Jornada: Rangeland Research Programs*. April 30, 2015. By Johnny Ramirez. https://jornada.nmsu. edu/blog/7-things-you-didnt-know-about-creosote-bush

93. **Phoenix Sentries**: "Ceremony at City Hall a Gesture of Progress" *The Arizona Republic*. October 21, 1929, p1. http://azcentral.newspapers.com/image/116957754/?terms=Cere mony%2BGesture%2Bof%2BProgress; "Courthouse - City Hall artistic addition to Phoenix skyline" *The Arizona Republic*. October 21, 1929, p17. http://azcentral.newspapers.com/ image/116957747/?terms=Courthouse%2B-%2BCity%2BHall%2Bartistic%2Baddition%2Bt o%2BPhoenix%2Bskyline

94. **Pioneer & Military Cemetery**: "Pioneer and Military Memorial Park" *City of Phoenix*. https://www.phoenix.gov/parks/parks/alphabetical/p-parks/pioneer

INDEX